BIGGER KIDS,
BIGGER PROBLEMS

So you survived adolescence and thought there
would be calmer waters ahead. Ha!

BIGGER KIDS,
BIGGER PROBLEMS

A Practical Handbook

by
Paul Avila Mayer CSW, PsyA
Sasha von Scherler CSW

A complete psychological program — parent friendly —
written for parents of kids over twenty-four —
presented in phases throughout the book.

GATES & BRIDGES

A Division of United Publishers Group
Norwalk, CT

Gates & Bridges
A Division of United Publishers Group Inc.
50 Washington Street
Norwalk, CT 06854

Library of Congress Cataloging-in-Publication Data
   is available.

ISBN: 0-8038-9412-0

Manufactured in the United States of America.

Dedication

We dedicate this book to the well-being
of our children and their
children and their children and
their children—
and yours.

Acknowledgments

We are profoundly grateful to Dr. Hyman Spotnitz for founding Modern psychoanalysis, to those inspiring scions of it, Don Shapiro, Ph.D. Jacob Kirman, Ph.D., Colette Linnihan, CSW, Nicole Kirman Ph.D., and Phyllis Cohen, Ph.D., and to the directors of the New York institutes where it is taught, William Kirman, Ph.D, Phyllis Meadow, Ph.D, and Judy Levitz, Ph.D..

We would like to express our thanks for the expertise and understanding of Dr. Terry Weill, M.D., a psychiatrist of wonderful wisdom, and Carol Brod, Ph.D, a warm and generous psychoanalyst. Both were kind enough to make suggestions we found invaluable.

Sasha wants to thank all the staff of Village Center for Care AIDS Day Treatment and, in particular, Bill Messina, CSW, Pat Rincon, CSW, and Tom Martin, CSW, MAT, for seven years of great collegiality. She also thanks Jan Zimmerman Rh.D, and Carmen Maldanado, CAC for conferring with her on nutrition and substance abuse.

We also thank Bernie Frankel, Ph.D., Dan Malamud, Ph.D. and in memoriam, Jean Zion, Ph.D. and William Hinckley Ph.D.

You may give them your love but not
your thoughts,
For they have their
own thoughts.

You may house their bodies but not their
souls, For their souls dwell in the
house of tomorrow,
which you cannot visit,
not even in your dreams.

You may strive to be like them,
But seek not to make them like you.

For life goes not backward nor tarries
with yesterday.

You are the bows
from which your children
as living arrows are sent forth.

— Kahlil Gibran
The Prophet (1923)

Contents

9

If Your Kid Might Be Gay, Or if You Are

10

Serious Illnesses — Including AIDS

11

When You Sell Used Cars and Your Kid Runs IBM — When You Are a Corporate Lawyer and Your Kid Is a Carpenter

12

If Your Kid Commits a Crime

13

If Your Kid Is Mentally Ill

How to Read This Book

This book presents a complete psychological system. Some parts of it will be new and, at times, unnerving. In contrast, other parts will seem no more than common sense, which indeed is all they are. Whether familiar or seemingly ridiculous, we recommend you give them a hearing. There are many ideas deliberately scattered throughout the book in order not to overwhelm the reader.

Read the Whole Book

Take your time. Think and feel and absorb. There will be chapters about problems with which you don't have to deal. Count your blessings and read them anyway. You may be surprised to find something in there for you.

And

If you can read this book without blowing your stack — #!*&!#!! and act on some of its suggestions we swear — no matter how rotten they've been — your relationships with your adult children will become, over time, more workable, more wonderful, and possibly more just plain fabulous — we mean more awesome — than you ever dreamed.

Introduction
For Still-Marrieds, Step-Families, Single Parents and Alternative Families

They are all grown up—*very* grown up sometimes—but to many of us, they are still our kids and we love them. Much of the time we're proud of them, amused by them, and delighted by them. But sometimes there are nagging feelings that are not so positive. Not always, but on occasion, we feel worried, sad, hurt, confused, depressed, disillusioned, bitter, frustrated, angry, several of the preceding, all of the preceding.

What happened? When they were little, there was this wonderful dream that after all the money, work, and heartache, we would have the joys of a warm, loving, mutually supportive family—in which our grown children would be blessings. And not that we should be crass, or anything, but many of us expected a successful family to boot.

It wasn't as if we didn't try. From the beginning of pregnancy, there were thousands of problems that required thousands of solutions. There always seemed to be something to do. Lamaze classes before they were born so their births would be easier, followed by all that getting up in the middle of the night, very often uncomplainingly, to nurse them or give them bottles. There were bumps and bruises and cuts and high fevers and real sicknesses and real injuries. Before we knew it, they were adolescents and we had games to attend and worries about the car. We did a thousand and one things for them. One of us was the father who faithfully carried his daughter's catsup bottle through some of the finer restaurants in France. Those of us who were lucky enough to live where there's a bit of grass had the dubious joy of running car pools. Those of us in big dangerous cities, driven by necessity to be cautious as hell, made complicated arrangements so children could get safely to school and safely home again.

All in all, as parents we spent years in service to our kids, and virtually no day was without a child's problem and a parent's solution. Most of those solutions were right or at least helpful. For over twenty years, we dealt with our children's difficulties. We got used to being helpful. We got used to being listened to. Many of us enjoyed the satisfaction of being a parent. It made us feel good to be needed and to solve problems.

As we struggled through the dreadful teenage years, we had to feel that there was light at the end of the tunnel, that our children were almost grown up and would soon take care of their own problems—look after themselves, be responsible, all of that. And some of us actually expected that they'd appreciate all that we did for them over the years.

That's what psychologists call "magic thinking." One example of magic thinking is an idea many of us had that at some specific age—eighteen, twenty-one, or even twenty-five—whichever number we'd picked as the age of liberation—our children would suddenly become competent, pleasing, self-fulfilling, and parent-gratifying young adults.

That isn't without some reason. Kids do become self-starting, often to a large extent. They want to get their lives going and function as adults, but they can't all get there right away. There are a lot of false starts. And if you're one of the fathers or mothers who feels that you've just traded in your kids and their kid problems for a bunch of grown-up children with grown-up problems, then you may find this book to be helpful.

It isn't that parents don't have answers. Many of our grown-up children's problems could be solved if they'd only listen to us and do what we tell them. The trouble is they won't. Why won't they? Somewhere along the line, we seem to have lost much of our authority. Many of our children turned us off during adolescence and haven't turned us on again, leaving us filled with the impulse to rush in and rescue, to provide advice, suggestions, help in any form we can think of.

THOMAS: Dad? I've got some bad news.
DAD: [Jumping to a conclusion] Are you all right?
THOMAS: [Testy] Don't I sound all right? [We're off on the wrong foot, already] No, it's the car. I guess you'd have to say it's totalled. [His car? Your car?]

LISA: Mom, are you sitting down?
MOM: What is it?
LISA: I'm late. Ten days.

Not easy situations.

They certainly weren't what we had in mind at the beginning. But there are almost always solutions, possibly not the old ones, possibly new ones instead.

This book is written with the profound conviction that things *can* get better, that relationships between parents and children *can* be rewarding. The techniques discussed in this book are psychoanalytic, and we think that while they might be unfamiliar, they might also make sense to you.

For those of you who are curious, the authors of this book have three adult children all in their early thirties at the moment of this writing. They are beautiful, self-actualizing, productive, warm, and generous children. We are profoundly grateful to have relationships with them that are all parents could ever ask for. But, during the sometimes turbulent years we have been through together, we have used many of the techniques discussed in this book to good advantage. We recommend them not only because we believe in them but also because we are grateful for them.

Beyond our own families, we have used these techniques successfully time and again with patients and their children. We are profoundly convinced that we are suggesting a way of working with adult children that offers hope to parents who are concerned about their kids.

But—and it's a big but—some of the recommended techniques are going to be difficult to accept; they will involve doing the very opposite of your impulses. Some of them may seem crazy to you; some of them will make you mad; but if you can open your mind to new approaches, if you can tolerate the ideas presented, we think you'll find them enormously helpful.

1

The Kids Who Can't Leave Home

All kinds of families, rich or poor, WASP, Asian, African American, Jewish, ethnic of your choice, gay, straight, upper-class, middle-class, lower-class, and déclassé, have children who can't leave home. Nasty economic conditions, toxic or enmeshed relationships in the family, and the new world-weary angst glue too many children to their childhood bedrooms.

No matter the reason, in much of today's society kids are not supposed to live in their parents' homes after they're grown. Rather they're supposed to go out and make their own way in the world, even if most of us hope they won't go very far.

Today, if our kids don't leave the family manse, parents are too often looked on as pathetic neurotics who raised weak, weird kids. Amateur psychologists nod their heads knowingly and say unpleasant things like: "Aha! Who in your family *unconsciously* wants Junior to stay at home?"

Parents don't need to hear such gratuitous suggestions from neighbors, hairdressers, grocers, or even from their own parents—

those myriad well meaning experts on raising other people's children. Why is it we always seem to be confronted with this problem on the day when a stocking has run, our roots are showing, or a spot was acquired on our necktie at breakfast? Something like this:

OLD COLLEGE
     FRIEND: [impeccably groomed]: Well, well, well, what's Junior doing?
        MOM: Uh, he's with us for the time being, packing up his model airplane collection . . .
OLD COLLEGE
     FRIEND: [snitty] No, I mean what's he doing?
        DAD: [avoiding answering] Fine, how's your Jennifer?
OLD COLLEGE
     FRIEND: [vicious] Oh she's just been appointed editor in chief of the *Miami Herald,* and her husband is taking over cancer research for the new administration, and their twins made the Baby Olympic swim team, and . . . but you don't just want to hear about Jennifer, our Chris as you may have seen in the papers has a new movie out, and his wife has just made *Fortune* 500 . . . and what did you say Junior was up to?
        MOM: [weakly] Junior we think is interested in aviation . . .

The problem is everywhere.

John[1] and Mary D. blew into our office from Westchester late one gusty February afternoon. They were a very successful

---

   1. Names and some data have been changed throughout this book to protect confidentiality.

African American couple who had really nailed the American dream. John, a hard working sportscaster, was a tennis-thin fifty-eight. Mary, his wife, at fifty-two looked many years younger than her age. Although she had been on a tenure track as a sociology professor, she had stopped working when Bill, their first and only child, was born, and didn't go back to work until he entered junior high school. John and Mary had wanted Mary to be able to raise their child. Their own mothers had had to work. Bill was to have the childhood his parents hadn't had.

And so he did. Bill went to the finest elementary and prep schools and attended an Ivy League college with a terrific allowance and even his own car. Why not? He was their only child.

But that afternoon in our office, John and Mary were beside themselves. Hurt and rage dominated as they told their story, but it was clear that above all they loved and cherished their son. Later, when they brought Bill in to see us, we could see why. He was a marvelous young man, tall, handsome, outgoing, affectionate, with a quick wit and a smile that would brighten any day. Why would anyone want this kid to leave home?

His mother said, "Because it isn't good for him—"

His father said, "When I think what I had to go through at his age—"

Twenty-six-year-old Bill had majored in postmodern philosophy. He was very good at burrowing in to the center of any question. When his parents said they were glad to be able to give him the time he needed to find himself, to identify a life's work that would be "meaningful," he replied, soulfully, "What is meaning?"

At that instant we felt the frustration John and Mary had been experiencing.

"Bill doesn't give a hot damn about things like professionalism, status, the future, and the idea that one must progress, get ahead, get farther than yesterday. He doesn't even give a damn about money, particularly mine," John raged.

It seemed the word "goal" was not part of Bill's vocabulary.

Phrases such as "there is no truth, all is relative" were.

At one point John shouted, "I'm terrified for your future!"

"Dad, look at the text of what you're saying," Bill replied. "Why do you put the word 'your' before 'future' when supposedly you're talking about 'my' future. Think about it Dad."

Unfortunately Mary enjoyed listening to Bill interpret the "text" when they tried to talk to Bill about his future. She sometimes couldn't help remarking on his cleverness.

John and Mary were growing apart.

It took a while after Bill's graduation before John and Mary began to wonder how much time they should give him to find "meaning." It was at just under the five-year point that they came to our office—angry and agitated.

In college Bill was interested in writing but decided not to pursue a career in writing until he had more life experience —meaning a wife and children—neither of which he acquired. Over time, Bill had many lovely girl friends, but whenever a girl began to get attached, he'd stop seeing her. As for writing, well, maybe he would and maybe he wouldn't. What was important, he said, was "to savor the now, live in the moment."

Bill savored the now and lived in the moment at home. John and Mary's home. By working as a substitute teacher, he made pocket money and saved to indulge his one passion—skiing. Each winter he went off for several months to various ski slopes around the country. Very often he worked as an instructor, which meant he could stay away longer. Late every spring, he always came home.

John lost patience first, which put him at odds with Mary, who still wanted to give Bill time. And time went on. Bill did work very hard during a political campaign for a small environmental party and wound up in a position of responsibility. John and Mary were thrilled. They were proud of their son. Mary recycled her already recycled garbage. John suggested a family trip rafting on the Colorado. "At last," beamed Mary, beamed John, "he's found himself."

Alas, when the campaign was over, Bill pronounced politics "a slimy business" and said he wanted nothing more to do with it. He also advised Mary and Bill never to eat fish again that came from lakes or rivers. Back to square one.

In the privacy of their bedroom, John raged and Mary sobbed while the tension mounted. John and Mary were at wit's end — with Bill and with each other. They didn't want to kick Bill out of the house, but they certainly wanted him to leave. They wanted him to grow up.

"What is grown up? Who is grown up, what is the measure of grown upness?" Bill questioned.

John and Mary felt they'd tried everything.

Foremost was patience. They'd given him five years in which to "find himself," with room, board and laundry thrown in.

Patience had segued into reasoning.

"Don't you ever want to AMOUNT TO SOMETHING?"

Apparently he didn't

"Settling down means burial to me," sighed Bill.

Reasoning gave way to arguing, which gave way to lectures. John provided good advice, straight from the shoulder — and it *was* good advice — without effect. Mary made some sensible suggestions, all of them equally ignored.

Lately Bill had been distant from his father and sulky with his mother. Sometimes he'd get tears in his eyes, and they could swear he was three years old again.

Finally they tried charging him rent.

He said, "Okay, okay, what does money mean? I'll give you all my money."

Only he didn't. He paid rent for one month and then skipped the next two.

John and Mary felt rotten. Their friends weren't making them feel any better talking about something called "tough love," which seem to mean "a good kick in the butt" or locking up his clothes until he paid his rent or, better yet, kicking him out of the house. John and Mary felt that if they followed their friends' advice they'd lose Bill. They didn't want to lose him. They wanted to help him.

Nothing had worked. Patience. Reason. Arguments. Suggestions. Monumental rage. John and Mary tried to get Bill to go to a therapist. He refused. In desperation, they came without him to our offices on that cold February afternoon—where they found an entirely new approach. At first they were a little horrified at what was presented to them but they were so desperate they agreed to give it a try.

To begin with, kids like Bill have a great capacity to divide their parents. Sometimes one parent will become the "good cop" and the other the "bad cop." In all instances, that's a bad business for parents. Kids like Bill are still wrestling with issues left over from childhood and adolescence, and one of the things they desperately need is for parents to be in agreement, to speak with one tongue. Bill had the habit of springing things on his mother in the kitchen or on his father outside the house, and before the other one knew it, one of them had agreed to something to which the other objected. And then there was real frustration in the house.

The first suggestion we made was that they work on speaking with one tongue. Life became easier when John and Mary had accepted how vital it was, whenever Bill made one of his loaded requests, to reply "Let me talk that over with your father" or "I'll have to talk to your mother about that." Only after the two of them had consulted and agreed could they speak with one tongue. And things began to improve around the house.

Okay, that was a beginning. But when John and Mary were finally united in dealing with their wonderful but infuriating son, what could they do next?

Bill was resisting living as an adult, real commitment, and success—all those good things. How could John and Mary eliminate that resistance so Bill could use his natural energies and gifts to get going, to make decisions, to start building a life for himself?

Psychoanalysts have learned over the years that attacking resistance makes it stronger. John and Mary knew that intuitively—but they didn't know what else to do. They'd noticed how little effect they'd had with all their reasoning, advising, arguing, shouting, and crying, but no one had showed them any other way of dealing with Bill. The reason their efforts came to nothing was that each of them was, in its own way, a frontal attack on Bill's resistance.

In our offices, we counseled John and Mary to do exactly the opposite of what they had been doing and urged them to "join" Bill's resistance. We advised them that when Bill wanted to sleep in late (at the risk of losing his teaching job) instead of trying to get him up or attacking him for being so irresponsible, when he finally did get up they should simply say something like "It must be good to sleep so long in the morning."

"Joining" is one of the principal psychological techniques we're going to recommend to you in this book, and it is not as easy to understand and execute as it might appear. It was certainly a most difficult recommendation for John and Mary to accept.

But since the old ways didn't work—and John and Mary knew they didn't—they agreed to try what seemed to them to be a crazy idea.

Joining Bill's resistance meant that the war was over. Whatever reward Bill was getting (what psychologists call the "secondary gain") from his resistant behavior was being taken away. The first noticeable change was that the tension in the household eased. John and Mary were busy joining Bill and were not so angry any more. They had something to do. Both of them were determined to keep on joining—to approve of whatever Bill did. Bill, of course, was unnerved by the inexplicable change, and his parents were surprised to see that he really wanted things back the way they'd been before. Bill began to increase his infuriating behavior, climaxing by getting himself fired from his job as a substitute teacher. John was delighted that he was able to say, "Oh, too bad. Well, you'll have more time for skiing."

Bill was having some trouble growing up. Through his behavior and his refusal to go out into the world, he really was saying to his parents, "I'm just a baby, and I need to be at home and be taken care of." Now his parents had joined the baby in him. Instead of getting mad, they made a great effort to try to remember the pleasure and excitement they felt when they brought him home from the hospital. With that memory in her head, Mary was able to tell Bill that she liked him home and dependent on her. (And, of course, there was more than a little truth in that.)

In our offices, we had stressed that joining wouldn't work unless it was genuine. If there was anger in John's voice, or sarcasm, or disapproval of any kind, the joining wouldn't work. If Mary's statement that she enjoyed having Bill at home and needing her wasn't genuine, it wouldn't work. In either case, there wouldn't have been real joining. The words might have been "Well, you'll have more time for skiing," but the emotion in John's voice would have carried the message "You're driving me crazy, and I'm furious at you." The words might have been "I like having you at home needing me," but the emotion in Mary's voice might have been saying "What can I do to get you to grow up?!" And neither of those would be joining. They would both be criticism, an attack on Bill's resistance, which would reinforce his resistance to growing up.

In order to be genuine in his joining, John had to think about skiing until he could find a part of himself that could imagine enjoying sliding down a snowy mountain slope. When he found that and could say with genuine understanding in his voice, "Well, you'll have more time for skiing" and not just sound as if he meant it but really mean it, then the results he wanted would follow. In the same way, in order for Mary to be genuine she had to admit that there was a part of her that did love Bill's dependency and allow those feelings to color her words.

Let's look a little more closely at what happened when John and Mary started joining Bill's resistance. In the beginning, Bill started by looking at his parents a little funny. He didn't get it. He knew something was changed, but he didn't understand what or why. And he didn't like it. What did he do? He set out to try to restore things to the way they were before. His responses grew stronger. He told his father he was trying to "con" him and admitted he was furious. As already noted, when his complaints didn't have any effect Bill redoubled his efforts to restore things to "normal" by losing his teaching job. That sent a shock wave through the house, but John and Mary hung in.

It wasn't easy for Bill's parents to join the resistance. But they wanted to do so—even though it was a struggle—and as part of that effort, they accepted a second recommendation.

It's an old psychological axiom that the only thing any of us can do for our kids is to be healthy ourselves. If John and Mary really wanted Bill to have a rich, full life they had to begin by having a rich, full life themselves.

Both John and Mary needed to focus more on outside activities which gave them pleasure. They came up with quite a long list—going to sports events together, enrolling in classes, joining a group, taking up jogging, seeing more friends—and began to work their way through the list. We encouraged them to get busy. No more hanging around the house trying to pretend everything was fine. Mary had taken a certain pleasure in cooking Bill's dinner and in the family's eating together. Now John and Mary made a point of going to dinner with friends and when that wasn't possible, they simply went out for pizza. John and Mary didn't rub it in; they just did it. They weren't out to punish Bill. Mary had always left a nice dinner on the stove for Bill when they were out. She stopped. Bill didn't have so much fun cooking and eating alone.

By enriching their own lives, John and Mary were giving Bill permission to enrich his. Without a word spoken.

Bill had been resisting his parents' efforts to help him grow up and behave responsibly, to act like an adult, and to be a success.

When his parents—by joining—made his resistance meaningless, he began the long process, on his own, without any further advice or prompting from them, to grow up, behave responsibly, act like an adult, and become a success. In Bill's case, it took the form of getting a full-time job in advertising and moving out of his parents' home.

It didn't happen overnight. After all, it had taken Bill twenty-five years to get into the mess he was in. But he made enough changes over a four-month period to encourage John and Mary to stick to their guns. When the big changes came—the full-time job and the moving out—they felt Bill was on his way. And curiously, instead of being angry at them for neglecting him (which was what Mary feared the most), Bill seemed to be happier with his new life and with them, which indeed he was.

There are countless variations on Bill's story—kids who can't leave home, kids who leave home but only go a short distance away and remain emotionally tied to home, kids who leave and come back, sometimes with small children, kids who go far away but have never really left. The data may be different but from a psychological viewpoint few of them are very different from Bill. And the remedies are often essentially the same. Let's look at some other examples.

What if the parent were a single, divorced mother (although it could easily have been a single, divorced father) and the problem was that the kid in question did leave home—and then didn't go very far away? And that single parent—fifty-four-year-old Marian—worried about her thirty-four-year-old daughter Betsy the way we all worry about our kids.

Marian had a lot to be proud of. From the time Betsy was a toddler, she was sweet and easygoing. She never caused any trouble, graduated in the upper third of her high school class, and went on to a local college. She had girlfriends and boyfriends and for a while was interested in college theater. Betsy's father had left when she was fourteen, but her mother, who had gone back to work a few months after Betsy was born, was able to support Betsy and herself on her salary.

After college, Betsy spent a few months at home, working as a secretary and saving her money before moving to her own small but sweet little apartment. The job didn't pan out—one of the men was harassing her—so she quit and found another job. That one wasn't quite right either, so after a few weeks she quit and found another. Finally she'd fallen into a way of life for herself. For the past twelve years she'd been working as a "temp," short for "temporary office worker."

Betsy said she liked the "newness" of a different work place every few days, which was quite brave considering that she was still really a rather timid person.

More and more, Marian had to admit she was worried because Betsy's life didn't seem to be going anywhere—and Betsy wasn't getting any younger. Why wasn't she married and having children? Or at least in a relationship? Why didn't she have a career, work that she found fulfilling? Why wasn't she happy?

Betsy lived alone in her sweet little apartment. She had a cat and a couple of girlfriends. Sometimes she would have a boyfriend, but after a few weeks or months he'd be gone. Betsy was quite pretty and attracting men seemed no problem. Keeping one of them was another matter. She often had "the blues."

Betsy phoned her mother twice a day and spent most of Saturday and Sunday with her—usually fighting. She found her mother bossy, intrusive, and overly involved with her. Betsy was driving her mother crazy with what seemed to be an almost willful refusal to go out into the world. Marian was a take-charge person, and she wanted Betsy to show some spunk. She thought Betsy too "easy" with men, lacking in "gumption." For her part, Betsy thought her mother was domineering and mean and that her life had been ruined when her father left. That accusation always hurt Marian deeply.

Now Betsy was a wounded pigeon, and her mother was having trouble sitting on all the anger and guilt rumbling around inside her. One thing making Marian so angry was the thought that Betsy was partly right, that if her parents had stayed together, if her mother had done something differently so that the marriage had lasted, then Betsy would have turned out better.

Betsy felt like a failure, and she was making her mother feel like a failure. They were both ferious.

We all know that family history can't be changed. There's no undoing the past. But we also know that it is possible to change the way people *feel* about the past, and changing the way people feel can change the rest of their lives.

Betsy and her mother were fighting because there was so much blaming going on. Marian blamed Betsy for not getting her life together, and Betsy blamed Marian for not teaching her how to do so and for the failure of her marriage.

The bad things that come from blaming are many. The good things that come from blaming are nil.

When Betsy's mother lost her temper and asked Betsy point blank "When are you going to make something of yourself?", Betsy became angry, petulant, and, in her own way, stubborn as hell. It's easy for us, as outside observers, to see that Marian's raging at Betsy wasn't doing either of them any good. Most of us know very well that "positive reinforcement," (supporting the strengths of a child), will produce far better results than "negative reinforcement" (blaming, criticism, scolding, and other forms of disapproval).

Understanding, support, approval, praise, and empathy make people feel better. They're empowering. But sometimes we lose our tempers and blame or criticize, and blaming and criticism cripple. The same goes for all those other horrors—nagging, scolding, and other forms of disapproval. They stunt our kids' growth. We take special umbrage at that thing called "constructive criticism." There is no such thing as constructive criticism. It is just criticism. And it cripples. It's very tempting to criticize.

When we're angry at a child, or frustrated, or disappointed, we get what's known as that "bad parent" feeling. We know things aren't working out the way we wanted, and we start out by blaming ourselves. But that gets too painful, so we blame the child instead. We get rid of all those bad parent feelings by dumping them on the child. The "bad child" feelings are easier to tolerate. Sometimes we yell; sometimes it's just a contemptuous look; sometimes it's sarcasm or scorn. It doesn't matter. They're all the same.

Criticism comes in all sizes and shapes and colors. We knew a young man whose mother was so profoundly disappointed in him she would look up and sigh when he came in the door. Do we have to tell you that he's an emotional cripple?

One of the most subtle ways of criticizing is by giving advice.

Even when people ask for advice, they usually don't want it. What they really want is to tell you the solution they've already worked out. Why would anyone like advice? It's almost always received as a put-down. It makes people feel that other people are smarter. Who wants to feel stupid?

How many times has someone asked you for advice and then argued with everything you said? Or simply ignored your every suggestion? And sometimes, when someone does take your advice, it feels like that person did so just in order to be able to come back later and complain. "I took your advice and look what happened to me . . . "

And that's when they ask for it.

It's *un*solicited advice that's the real villain.

Few things are as unwelcome as unsolicited advice. But we all suffer from the urge, and we can all remember, to our chagrin, occasions when we couldn't control the impulse to rush in and tell someone else what to do.

Most of the time, we're not even aware of what we're doing. We're so anxious to help—or simply so anxious—that with what we consider the best intentions in the world we hurry in and do the wrong thing. We say . . .

"You know what might help . . . "
"Why don't you . . . ?"
"What about . . . ?"

And each of those suggestions says to the other person . . .

"You're not able to figure things out for yourself, so I'll tell you
    what to do . . . "
"I'm smarter than you are. Let me show you."
"The solution is obvious, and you're too dumb to see it, so here
    it is . . . "

The real message in unsolicited advice is: "you're stupid."

Betsy was resisting all her mother's efforts to improve her.
Despite the arguing and the fighting, she remained an isolated
young woman, unable to get the things she wanted for herself. In
a thousand ways, Marian pointed out the errors of Betsy's ways
using blaming, criticism, and the hated unsolicited advice. It is
true that, like John and Mary, Marian had noticed that none of
the things she was doing was bringing about the changes she
wanted, but she went on anyway. What else could she do?

Well, there was something else: a "power talk" with Betsy.

You probably think that we're referring to Marian's power to
bring about changes in Betsy. But, actually, it's Betsy's power
we're talking about. The trick is to recognize that as parents we're
often powerless, and it's our kids' own powers that must be ener-
gized. It's awful to think that as parents of grown children we're
powerless. But instead of treating our powerlessness as a negative
and blaming ourselves and wrestling with a huge sense of failure
and guilt, we have to make a positive out of it. We've recognized
a truth. We're powerless. Being realistic is an important beginning, even though it makes us feel bereft at first.

What can we as powerless parents do? What could Marian do?
Betsy seemed so passive and stubbornly unwilling to change.

Marian had become so desperate that she persuaded Betsy to enter family therapy with her. Betsy went twice and then dropped out. Marian stayed in treatment. In the sessions that followed the idea emerged that Marian could have a power talk with Betsy. To prepare Marian, we told her it was vital that no criticism slip into her voice. She would not be ready to have a power talk until she had previously vented all her negative feelings so that she would only express truly genuine concern and love for Betsy. In no way would she express any criticism of Betsy for failing to get her act together. Betsy needed to hear that her mother felt like a failure as a parent because apparently something had gone wrong and her mother had failed to teach her how to be a success. *Marian had to be very sure of the fact that in a power talk the parent must hand over all power to the child.* The parent must announce absolute powerlessness in the child's life. Then, and only then, can the parent go on to express her emotional truth to her child without blaming, criticizing, or giving advice.

Marian's power talk with Betsy took place in Betsy's kitchen. In that session, she told Betsy that she was very concerned about her, that she loved her, thought she deserved a rich, full life, and felt powerless to help her get that rich, full life.

Since Betsy was already feeling like a failure, it relieved her to know that her mother was feeling the same way. Betsy felt understood, and she and her mother experienced a sad–happy coming together as they realized they both felt like failures.

That was the beginning. The way was now opened for Marian to ask Betsy about her life. And now Marian needed to listen.

Betsy told her mother that she was frightened, that she felt terrible about not being able to establish a real relationship, and that sometimes she was very sad. It was difficult for Marian not to leap in at that point with a suggestion, but she somehow managed not to do so. Instead, she tried to be empathic.

Empathy is not sympathy. Sympathy is essentially demeaning. Empathy is not compassion. Compassion makes people feel little and condescended to. Empathy is simply feeling the same feelings as the other person and acknowledging them. When Betsy admitted to feeling frightened, sad, and helpless, it wasn't very hard for her mother to feel frightened with her and sad with her and helpless like her. Almost any empathic remark, recognizing Betsy's feelings, would be helpful.

We had recommended "Ummmmmm" or "Ohhhhhh" as the very best empathic responses. But some others are . . .

"Being frightened is a terrible way to feel."
"It must be awful being sad so much of the time."
"Feeling helpless is the pits."

That's empathy and it will move mountains.

What Marian actually said, with honest feeling in her voice, was, "You've been really suffering."

Betsy felt understood and burst into tears.

Notice that Marian did not talk about herself. She didn't say:

"I feel frightened for you, myself."
"Looking at you makes me so sad."
"Listening to you makes me feel so helpless."

Please notice that each of those statements could have been received as a criticism, as Marian informing Betsy that her problems were upsetting her mother. Fortunately, thanks to the work she had been doing in therapy, Marian didn't blame or criticize. She spoke about Betsy and Betsy's feelings, and Betsy felt understood. She knew there'd been a change, that her mother wasn't blaming her, criticizing her, or telling her what to do. In spite of the depressing nature of their talk, Betsy was not in the least depressed; in fact, she was feeling distinctly better.

Marian, who had been working hard in therapy, now added a little joining, saying, "It doesn't sound like there's anything you can do." And then she turned over all the power to Betsy: "Well, listen, you're a grown woman now, and I expect you'll find your own answers. You know I'm here for you. If there's anything you want from me, all you have to do is ask."

Betsy's mother gave Betsy the power to take charge of her own life, to make her own decisions. Marian relinquished her parental power. That's empowering for Betsy. That's why this was called a power talk.

This was a story with a happy ending. (And, in all fairness, it must be admitted that not every situation that comes into a therapist's office is successfully resolved.) But Betsy seemed to take some sort of renewed energy from the change in the way her mother was treating her. Perhaps the energy she had been using to fight with her mother was released now to be used for her own purposes.

Betsy decided she wasn't ready to be married but that she was ready for a real "relationship." When the next man came into her life, she began to invest in the relationship, which then flourished. Betsy is now living with the new man, and they are considering whether marriage is a possibility for them. Whatever their decision, Betsy has taken a great step forward. She has given up the child–mother relationship with Marian and has become her grown daughter instead. Marian is enormously relieved. She is nothing but hopeful about the future. Her new positive feelings make it easy for her to continue substituting joining and empathy for all those wild impulses to blame or criticism or rush in and give advice.

But what if the difficulties arise in a dysfunctional family, one troubled with alcoholism, emotional illness, and a chaotic marital history? And what if the kid who didn't really leave home is living far away? If the grown child of a family hasn't separated, hasn't become his own person with his own goals and dreams but is still living the life of a child to whom the goals and dreams of father and mother are all important, then we say that he has not truly left home. He is merely living at a distance.

Tom was the thirty-two-year-old child of such a family, living eight hundred miles from home. In the photographs his father showed us, Tom was tall and handsome, and, according to his father, he was a delightful companion, a great talker with big plans and bigger dreams. Yet those who were close to him knew him to be chronically unhappy, always searching for better feelings in something new, and inevitably disappointed.

Tom's mother had died when Tom was eight. After the funeral, she was rarely mentioned again. Tom's father, George, a hard-driving, hard-drinking bond salesman, assumed from the way his son talked that he was self-starting and independent, but that didn't seem to be the case. For the last several years in particular, George had been trying to set Tom straight with a series of letters expressing his confidence and his conviction that once Tom got his life untangled he'd go "right to the top" in whatever field he selected. Then, of course, those letters would provide suggestions on things Tom could do to go "right to the top."

George came to our offices about quite a different subject, his chronic depression. But much of his depression seemed to be connected with Tom, and our hearts did go out to him.

One difficulty was that Tom never selected a field in which to go "right to the top." By the time Tom was thirty-two, he'd been living in a mid-western city three states away, working as a bus boy, which made George feel crazy. For Tom's birthday, George'd sent him a check and a graduate school catalog. Tom never acknowledged either, although he cashed the check.

Tom never seemed to finish things. In school, he could get good grades any time he tried. Of course, he didn't always try. Girls liked him and he liked girls, but somehow he was always moving on to someone new. In high school, he drank too much but never enough to be called a drunk. In college—he managed to get through three years—he experimented with all the drugs, more so than some of his classmates, but he never became a "druggie."

From his first days in grade school, it was taken for granted by the family that Tom would be an artist. He could always draw, and he seemed interested in pursuing art. George thought he could do well as a commercial artist. But in college Tom got into computers and might have followed through on that interest if he hadn't dropped out.

After school he half-heartedly tried acting. He usually supported himself by driving a taxi. Sometimes he asked for money from his father, but mostly he barely got by.

As far as relationships went, George was always puzzled. Sometimes Tom had a girlfriend; sometimes he'd go for months without seeing anyone his family knew about. He just didn't attach himself to anyone or any place. He floated from city to city, even to foreign countries. In his late twenties, he developed romantic ideas about Asia, but his year in Japan seemed to consist mostly of mooching off his friends. The most recent eight months as a bus boy were his longest stint of work. When he called home (he never wrote; he phoned collect), he talked about "going to the coast," although it wasn't clear if he meant the East Coast or the West Coast. George suspected it wasn't clear to Tom, either. Actually, George was upset by that call and replied with a blistering letter, which he mailed before showing it to his therapist.

Tom was another grown kid who hadn't been able to find a life for himself. George was increasingly worried about him, and, despite the fact that his tactics hadn't worked in the past, he was persisting in those tactics, even more intensely.

Would George ever figure Tom out? Tom wasn't telling him in words, but he was certainly telling him in actions. Tom had been moving farther and farther from home. That had to say something. Tom had been putting his message into clear language ("I'm thinking of moving to the coast"), but George couldn't hear what he was saying. What did it all mean? Well, one way to understand it was to suspect that Tom was hurt or angry or both.

George needed to be responsive to his son's feelings of hurt and anger, but so far he'd only been involved in his own worries about Tom that he hadn't been able to tune in to the boy. Despite the long history of Tom's ignoring his father's unsolicited advice, George had persisted in advising, suggesting, and criticizing, in letter after letter, especially when he'd been drinking. Their relationship was like a train heading downhill without brakes. Big trouble ahead. George's actions had been systematically alienating Tom for years.

George was in real danger of losing his son.

He had been pouring forth a steady barrage of letters which, while loving and concerned, contained regular doses of criticism, blaming, and unsolicited advice. The love and concern in those letters went virtually unrecognized, but the criticism, blaming, and unsolicited advice remained with Tom like red-hot coals burning away inside him.

There was so much alienation between George and Tom that a power talk wasn't possible. Tom would only receive what his father said as more criticism and blaming and unsolicited advice.

Finally, after quite a long time, George's depression reached the point where he could not only ask his therapist for a suggestion but listen to the answer. We suggested to him that there was a way for George to change the dynamics between himself and his son, but it was a difficult way.

First he would have to accept his own powerlessness. He could not impact on his son. He wanted desperately to help Tom, to straighten him out, but there was nothing he could do. In his frustration George'd already been doing exactly the opposite of what was good for Tom—blaming and criticizing and offering unsolicited advice.

It was about this time that George came to terms with his own alcoholism and began, rather tentatively to explore a 12-Step Program (see chapter 3) concurrent with his therapy. Among the first lessons he learned was his own powerlessness over other people, including his son.

When George had sadly accepted his own powerlessness, he was able take the next step. He found the self-control, the self-discipline to do nothing—because anything he did would alienate Tom further.

We recommended that all letters had to stop. Instead, he was to begin a series of judiciously spaced phone calls, once a month, twice a month, whatever he sensed Tom could tolerate. Each of those phone calls was to be brief. Each was limited to expressions of love and support—"Listen, I love you and I'm for you . . . "—and nothing more. If there were some family news that wouldn't be inflammatory, George could pass it along. Questions like "What're you up to?" or even "What's new?" had to be avoided because George realized they sounded to Tom like . . .

"So, you accomplishing anything yet?"

"You finally getting your act together?"

By pulling back, George was giving Tom's wounds a chance to heal. In the past, he'd been pulling off the scab with each new letter. By not writing, by not asking inflammatory questions, he eliminated the blaming, the criticism, and the unsolicited advice.

We worked with George to help him understand that whatever Tom was doing was going to be fine with him. That was joining. And George's steady support for whatever Tom was feeling was empathy.

Over time, after Tom had learned that his father wasn't going to hurt him anymore, he was able to come home for a visit and begin to address the issues of choosing a life for himself. Tom is now in college, completing his final year. He is hoping to make some decisions before he graduates. George is so relieved that sometimes he feels like crying.

2

Fateful Returns: The Kids Who Come Back

We'd like to present another example of children who can't leave home—an even more startling form of this phenomenon—the child who *returns* home, sometimes with small children, a year, two years, even five years after the original departure. And the returnee clearly expects all rights and privileges.

We had close personal friends who went through this experience in a most distressing way. The suggestions we made to them were specific to their situation, but they apply to many others.

It was 3:00 A.M. one Sunday morning when two of our oldest actor friends, Jan M. and Doug A., called and asked us to get down to their apartment immediately. "No one is dead," said Jan in that whisper that could fill a theater, "but hurry."

When we arrived Jan passed six-week-old Gracie and a bottle to me. "We need you to sit with Miranda's babies while we take her to the hospital." Two-year-old Max was asleep on the couch. Miranda looked as if she had a dislocated shoulder. Her face was a mass of purple and yellow discoloration. There were rakelike scratches on her arms and legs. Obviously she had been beaten. Beautiful, exquisite, elfin Miranda. She gazed up at me, "Oh, Aunt Sasha, it's all my fault. I was bad. I made him mad. I wasn't good."

I could feel Paul stiffen as I did. Miranda was not just physically ill. This bright and glorious girl was mentally ill as well. (See chapter 11 on dealing with mental illness.)

What had happened?

Jan and Doug are primarily stage actors. Almost every season they had appeared off or on Broadway or guest-starred with a regional acting company—even though the theater kept shrinking, and they kept getting older. Luckily their stage earnings were shored up by soap opera contracts, commercials, and the odd film or two shooting in New York. So they managed to make stage careers and living in New York seem lucrative and glamorous long after both were neither.

They had a small but exquisitely furnished apartment, wore superb but understated clothes (Jan knew how to get theater seamstresses to make and alter things for the proverbial song), and Miranda never noticed the strain. Somehow Doug and Jan made an actor's life look fun and luxurious, concealing the great care it took.

Miranda was the perfect fun addition to their life, a precious little girl to have English high tea with, to costume, to read to, or to just plain adore. Jan and Doug were canny at shopping and making goodies stretch. One way or another, Miranda had the best of everything from party shoes to orthodontists, and at the best prices.

Indispensable to Doug, Jan, and Miranda in maintaining their lifestyle was their rent-controlled apartment. Although it had only one bedroom, there was no question of moving when Miranda was born. "When you have a living room and a Queen Anne gateleg table, who needs a dining room?" gaily queried Jan in an interview in the Arts and Leisure section of the *New York Times*. "We've made Miranda her own little stateroom of a bedroom," said Doug waving grandly at their erstwhile "dining alcove," which served as Miranda's bedroom throughout her childhood.

When Miranda came home in May of her sophomore year at Yale, declaring she wanted to marry a fellow classmate the minute school was out, they managed a small but correct wedding followed by an impeccable reception at the Player's Club. The fact that Miranda was just a bit pregnant didn't worry them unduly. She could finish college later. After all, the boy was from a good family and had already been offered a job in a bank training program. After the reception, Doug threw his hat in the air and said to Jan, "That's it, darling! We've done our all for Miranda, and now it's our turn!"

Jan replied, "We'll be careful and finish the cabin and spend more and more time up there, and, oh, darling, we'll have a dining room again!"

"Without the Yale bills, I can stop using hair dye, worrying about that five pounds that always wants to get me, and just be a character man. At last. It's hard passing for a juvenile after forty years. I'm going to forget that face-lift."

"Well, I've already had my lift, and my hair will always be yellow rather than white. But lambkin, let's face it, work isn't what it used to be." Jan was right; male actors' earnings drop precipitously at fifty-five, and women's decline at forty-two.

Years ago, they had bought an old fishing lodge on a lake in the Adirondacks. It really wasn't more than a shell, but it was in magnificent country. Whenever they could spare the money and the time from auditions, they worked on the cabin, gutting it, rebuilding it, and winterizing it. Doug built cherry cabinets. Jan made curtains and quilts. It was their toy, their treat, possibly even their retirement home.

To make a long story short, Miranda's marriage had been awful almost from the start. She became an abused wife fairly quickly, and her parents were not aware of it. (See chapter 13 on abusive relationships.) Now Miranda was back home with two infants, just after Jan and Doug had gotten things together for themselves—but they had no extras to contribute to her.

It was dawn before Jan and Doug returned to relieve us of our babysitting. Doug stormed into the apartment shouting. Jan was fluttering behind him, as shocked at what he was saying as we were. He who had hardly ever raised his voice at Miranda, who had been the most indulgent of fathers, was now raging at her. "Well, what am I supposed to do if she is such a dumb cow to have gotten herself hooked up with such a bastard? All right, Jan, now what?"

Jan couldn't get in a word.

"So now we live in this apartment with two screaming babies and diapers hanging from the ceiling? Perhaps if I become a waiter I might be able to support this shebang. Oh, I know, you want me to sell the cabin!"

"I never said any such thing—Doug—please—don't—"

"You thought it, Jan. I heard you!"

"Doug, our child is lying in a hospital bed and is, what did they say? clinically depressed—"

"Well, she'll have to get herself together—"

Doug couldn't stop raging.

"Time out!" cried Paul.

We persuaded Jan and Doug to go to bed and get some sleep. We all agreed to meet the next day.

There were so many problems to be faced. Miranda's babies needed care—including their mother's availability. Miranda needed care, both physical and psychological. Then there were the problems of her legal status, her lack of money, her safety vis à vis her husband, and of her children's safety.

At the moment, it seemed she was too sick to go anywhere but to her parents after being released from the hospital. They saw the problems and were rallying around. But there were two other major problems Doug and Jan really weren't seeing—which also had to be addressed.

The first problem was their emotional responses. Doug's rage and Jan's depression, produced by the sudden new stress, would play a major role in the outcome of the situation. The second problem, obviously, was how long Miranda and her babies would be living with them in that tiny apartment.

Jan had asked us for help. We were extremely hesitant. Using professional skills with friends was a good way to lose the friends. But since we couldn't say "no" to Jan, we cautiously agreed to do what we could.

The next day Miranda was released from the hospital. She was depressed and couldn't stop crying; she was also afraid that her husband would try to steal her children.

That evening Doug and Jan came up to dinner with us. They were fighting. Doug was furious that Jan couldn't see how terrible it was to have Miranda and the babies with them. His nightmare was that they would never leave. Jan was bewildered and shocked. Doug had never been so ungallant in the thirty years she had known him.

Paul said, "You can't deal with any of this until you come to terms with your own feelings."

"Stop that goddamned psychological claptrap with me, Paul. I'm sick of hearing you spout that damned stuff. Here I am one of the best damn actors I know. I should be playing Lear now. Will you tell me where the parts are? I've had contract after contract. I've been a spokesperson. And now they're throwing me away. Next. Next. Thank you very much, next . . . "

We were all quiet while Doug let out all the frustration he had about his career, the anger he had never expressed at Miranda for not finishing Yale. His anger went back into her childhood. He had never let himself feel the resentment he had felt at what she cost. He'd had to stay in New York where he could do soap operas and commercials to support their lifestyle.

That evening, for the first time ever, Doug expressed how furious he was that he had never had the chance to try Hollywood because he and Jan believed it was better for Miranda to be brought up on the East Coast. Then the cabin. Now, to support Miranda and the babies, he might have to lose it. And what about that bastard, his son-in-law . . . ?

It was a long while before he slowed down. Then, almost as if he were waking up, he stopped, shook his head and looked around, saying, "Sorry I just couldn't stop."

Jan and I went out to the kitchen.

"Will you help us, please? You know we haven't money to go to anyone." She was crying.

"Of course we will."

"I hated it in there just then, when he was so angry."

"Jan, it's good for him to vent all that anger. Can you get him to take walks and just rage till he gets it out?"

"I've never been comfortable with Doug's black moods."

"What will happen if he has the black moods?"

"Nothing I suppose."

"Why don't you go in and tell him you hate it, too."

"But I don't. Miranda is my child."

"Can you honestly say you want her to come home battered, with two children, no job, and emotionally ill?"

"I still couldn't say I hate it."

"Well, you're an actress. Could you act it?"

"I hate it! I can't bear it!" screamed Jan running back to the living room. "Doug, you're right. We are going to go out of our minds. And now when we should have a little more of a nest egg we'll have to be spending everything on Miranda . . ."

"Now it's not that bad. Come on darling, Miranda is our little girl. We'll take care of her like we always have. We can handle a small mortgage. Together, love, we can do anything."

The power of joining. Jan had supported Doug's anger and he was able to let go of it and in turn help Jan with hers.

One venting and one piece of joining, of course, wasn't going to be enough.

Paul spoke up.

"Look, this is a bad situation and it looks like it'll go on for a while. What about you two coming to us for dinner on Sunday nights for the next few weeks and we'll try to be helpful?"

What they would need was a regular emotional outlet, and for the moment, we seemed the best choice. Helping them put feelings into words was easy. Dealing with Miranda wouldn't be so easy. She would need a therapist who specialized in battered women, a lawyer, possibly an order of protection from the police, and some long-term help. She would have to get her life in order and move out of Doug and Jan's apartment.

But the first signs of serious emotional problems had already appeared. Miranda was curiously happy to be home. She was like a little girl again and didn't want to even talk about moving out. It was nice to have Mommy helping with the kids.

In the next six weeks much was done.

We found Miranda a therapist with a low fee who specialized in battered women. Miranda's husband got in touch with her, and, when she refused to return to him, he became threatening. All of that had to be dealt with through lawyers and the police.

Miranda's physical injuries healed, but the psychological wounds remained. The closeness of five people in a tiny apartment—where it had taken extraordinary love and accommodation for three people to survive long ago—was intolerable.

Doug and Jan were still coming to our house each Sunday night, when Doug had an opportunity to put into words all the intense feelings he was having. That was helping. But when was Miranda going to start taking charge of her life? She certainly showed no signs of doing so.

Miranda had become their little girl again, bright-eyed, eager, pleasing, and delighted for them to make all the decisions. She was resisting being a grown up, resisting taking responsibility for her own life and for her children. The time came when we thought that problem could be addressed.

Sasha asked Jan if she had any of Miranda's toys stored anywhere.

"As a matter of fact, I do, up in the cabin. Two big cartons we threw things into for years."

We recommended joining, which took a lot of persuasion. When Doug and Jan finally grasped what we meant, they went up to the cabin and brought back Miranda's toys. Jan then began to enjoy the baby in Miranda. They did the same things they had done years before. There were tea parties. Old costumes came down from a high shelf so that they could play dress up. Sometimes they read together. Doug entered into the joining, referring to Miranda as "my little girl."

Because they were actors Doug and Jan were really successful at making the joining genuine.

At first Miranda loved being treated as a baby, but after a couple of weeks she began to protest. Doug and Jan didn't seem to notice her protests. Miranda began looking for an apartment. They assured her that wasn't necessary. Miranda became insistent. Reluctantly, they agreed to help her look. As they searched for an apartment, Miranda became more adult, negotiating with landlords on her own without help from either of her parents. When they found an apartment only two blocks away, she was delighted and began looking for child care and a job.

The irrational component in Doug's anger was gone. He was pleased with the way Miranda was getting herself together. He and Jan worked on their budget and found they could set aside some money each month to help with her expenses, and they both agreed to babysit when they could.

Miranda and the two babies stayed with Doug and Jan for a total of nine weeks, which was long enough. And there were many other ramifications of Miranda's problems, as can be seen in chapters 11 and 13. But by being responsive to their own feelings and joining Miranda in hers, Doug and Jan had greatly improved a most troublesome situation.

The techniques we are showing you are simple and, if they're used correctly, can be remarkably effective.

3

Family Wars

Ope of the most painful situations we've all had to struggle with is the family war. Like real wars, family wars are big and small, skirmishes and grand battles. At their worst, these wars produce pain and loss, and when there is a "victory" it's often at great cost, frequently in the seeding of a future war.

We want to encourage the idea that we can't think our way out of emotional battles, but we can often feel our way out. A war within the family results in emotional problems, and the solutions are almost always emotional solutions. We should feel our way out of these situations, using emotional energy to find ways to make things better. We believe passionately that problems *can* be solved. Not every problem, not every time, but *many* problems *many* times.

But let's start with a small war.

Consider the entanglement over Nathan's dog.

Beauty, an adorable, shapeless, little puppy, was given to Nathan by his sister, Adele. Neither Adele nor Nathan gave any thought to the fact that his apartment's lease prohibited pets.

In four months, the adorable, shapeless, little puppy who had never been outside the apartment had grown into a big, bouncy Malamute who had to be walked four times a day—and the landlord soon cornered Nathan and suggested Beauty had to go, possibly with Nathan still holding the leash.

Nathan loved his apartment, and his efforts to find a place where he could keep Beauty were half-hearted. He decided to leave Beauty temporarily with Adele, who was working at home that summer, while he looked for a new place.

Adele woke up one October morning—when Beauty had been with her for nine weeks—and realized it had been a month since she had heard from her brother. When she phoned, she got his answering machine, and Nathan didn't return her calls. Adele finally called their mother in a fury, demanding help in finding the recalcitrant Nathan. It was a grand muddle. Nathan was angry at Adele for giving him an animal she knew would cause him to lose his apartment. Adele was mad at Nathan for abandoning Beauty with her. Their mother was mad at them both for behaving like children and requiring her, in the middle of a busy schedule, to deal with their problems.

There were many strong feelings, but no relationships were threatened. Instead, this little war served the purpose of keeping these three people entangled with each other, at no great cost to any of them. Mother and both children were all high-functioning, independent, self-supporting, essentially autonomous people. But each of them feared separation from the others.

This nice little war—which was only one in a series of brother-sister conflicts in which the mother served as the arbiter—made them feel close to one another, involved and cared about and needed. A lovely little war.

Other wars can be far less benign.

Consider Arthur David, or "A. D." as he was known, his wife Beth, and their three children, Alexander, Fletcher, and Joanne. When A. D. was little, he was taught that boys are brave, don't cry, and never admit they're in pain. In A. D.'s family, showing emotion was considered unmanly. A. D. grew up to be tall, good-looking, and hard-working, an amiable man who got along well in the corporate jungle. (He's in insurance and does very well.) By always being pleasant—and a little remote —he climbed the corporate ladder. He thought he was a success as a husband and father as well because he was always reasonable. Oh, sometimes he wondered why he didn't seem to feel things very deeply. But he didn't wonder very often.

A. D.'s wife, Beth, was raised by an emotionally needy mother who hadn't been able to be truly nurturing. Beth was comfortable with A. D., probably because he left her feeling emotionally starved, as had her mother.

In the first flurry of courtship and the early years of marriage A. D. had made an extra effort and managed to appear reasonably warm and loving. His sexual interest in Beth had driven him to extend himself. But as the years passed, A. D. lapsed back into his amiable if remote self. He provided a nice home in a nice neighborhood and that seemed to him enough.

When A. D. and Beth's children were born, he felt a surge of pride. Deep inside, he loved his children, but he had no idea how to express the loving feelings that lurked within.

Only after A. D. and Beth had been married for several years did Beth take stock. She noted the decision by A. D.'s family to reject "Arthur," "Art," or the more cozy "Artie"; or the possibilities of "David," "Dave," or "Davie" and select instead the antiseptic initials A. D. Beth concluded that early decision had reflected the family's desire for impersonal relationships. She found herself concerned but unsure what to do.

As time passed, Beth had become more and more concerned both for A. D. and herself and for their children. By this time, their three children were really grown. Of the three, it was Alexander who seemed most to resent his father's remoteness.

The first-born son, Alexander's feelings about A. D. were complicated from the beginning. He loved A. D. because he was his father and he certainly wanted his approval and appreciation. But at the same time, Alexander bitterly resented what he experienced as his father's deliberate withholding of love. The seeds of war were sown early.

In fact, the same drama was repeated for both father and son throughout Alexander's childhood. Alexander would be drawn to his father out of love and neediness. A. D. would recognize that Alexander wanted something from him, want to give it to him, and not know how. In his frustration he would become distant or gruff, and Alexander would wind up brooding over hurt feelings.

Alexander had many of his father's qualities. For one thing, he never expressed his anger at his father. He would keep approaching him —

"Hey, Dad, can I help you?"
"Dad, you want to come to the game on Saturday?"
"Could I ask you something, Dad?"

—and A. D. always responded "correctly" to Alexander. He would say—

"Sure."
"Yes."
Or "You bet."

But what would follow was invariably unsatisfactory.

If A. D. let Alexander "help," the boy would be clumsy or inept, and A. D. would start to worry about his tools and then become impatient or critical. Alexander would wind up feeling he never could do anything right, and his father's feelings weren't really so different.

If A. D. went to the game on Saturday, he wouldn't show enough interest or wouldn't praise Alexander the way the boy needed to be praised. After the game, in spite of A. D.'s attendance, they would both be disappointed.

Or if Alexander asked his father a question, the answer would be too complicated, and the boy would give up too soon, making his father feel inadequate.

In all of these situations A. D. kept missing the point. Alexander didn't want to help his father, get him to go to the game, or get him to answer a question. In every instance, the boy was really asking to be closer to his father. But A. D. didn't know how to be close to anyone.

After Alexander went off to college the heavy fighting began. During his visits home, he began demanding the intangibles he wanted—and demands closed A. D. right down. The two began to fight in earnest, each out of his own frustration. A. D. was damned if he'd give in to his son's demands, which the older man couldn't understand. In turn Alexander pulled back, and his visits home became even less frequent.

By the time he was twenty-five, Alexander and his father were estranged. A talented singer, Alexander was living in Los Angeles. His rare visits home would end up in shouting matches and were always about the wrong things. He and his father would shout about what kind of car Alexander should buy. They would fight about how seldom he came home and how his long absences hurt his mother. A. D. would denigrate Alexander's decision to become a musician; Alexander would rage over his father's lack of respect.

In short, they seemed to fight about everything except what they were really fighting about, A. D.'s inability to meet Alexander's needs for closeness, love, and approval. A. D. was never able to tell his son that *he* missed him because he wasn't aware he had those feelings. All he wanted was for Alexander to acknowledge that A. D. had done his best—which Alexander would never do.

When Alexander informed his family he wouldn't be home for Christmas that year, A. D. was very upset and recognized that he was feeling unhappy. That was a revelation because A. D. didn't normally deal in emotions like happiness or unhappiness. Terrified by the realization that he was feeling something, A. D. agreed to go with Beth to a psychotherapist in order to try to understand why Alexander was behaving so badly.

After listening to A. D. and Beth in a couples session, we suggested that they both have individual sessions each week and a joint session every two weeks. There was a lot to do.

In A. D.'s first individual session, he was asked to identify his own goals. At first, he thought that his only goal was to bring his son to his knees, to force Alexander to admit that his father had been doing everything he could and that Alexander had been making unfair demands.

But when A. D. listened to himself, he didn't like the sound of what he was saying. After further exploration and considerable pain, he decided instead that his goal was to have a loving relationship with his son, even if he didn't know what those words meant.

To achieve that goal something had to change. A. D. finally admitted he'd be willing to lose the family war if it would help him reach that goal. We encouraged his surrender. Instead of trying to force Alexander to bend to him, he himself was to bend to Alexander. A. D. was a proud man and that wasn't easy for him to do.

In our work, however, as he began to explore his own role in the war, he came to see that blaming and criticism had been driving Alexander away. For the first time, A. D. felt bad—which was again good because he was having feelings—and bad because they were uncomfortable feelings. The end result was that he decided to accept our recommendation that he lose the war.

That change in attitude on A. D.'s part paved the way for everything that followed. In our offices we explored what "losing the war" might actually mean. We rehearsed what he might say to Alexander and what Alexander might say to him.

When he felt he was fully prepared, A. D. called Alexander and asked if it would be all right for him to come to Los Angeles for a visit. Just father and son. Alexander was very moved by his father's actually asking to visit him.

On the day A. D. arrived in California, he asked Alexander take him to places where he studied, worked, and hung out. A. D. refrained from saying he thought Alexander's friends were weird. In fact, A. D. made a huge effort to accept everything he was shown without being negative.

The crisis came later that night, in Alexander's apartment. This was a moment of great temptation. A. D. felt a huge urge to unburden himself—to tell his son about his own difficulties with feelings and of his visits to the therapist. Fortunately, he was able to resist that impulse, which would have been, basically, a defense, a restatement of his own position that he had done the best he could, a subtle renewal of the war. He was determined to surrender.

Instead, using a form of joining, A. D. said he felt his son had some things to say to him and he had come to Los Angeles to hear them. He invited Alexander to explain to him again what he had done wrong as a father. It took considerable encouragement before Alexander believed what his father was saying and was willing to express the angry feelings he had inside. After all, he was his father's son and had been trained not to express angry feelings directly. But once he began—and realized that his father wasn't responding with an attack the way he usually did—he found he could go on. And on and on.

Alexander talked from 11:15 P.M. until 3:20 A.M. He poured out, in increasing detail and with increasing feeling, every grievance he had ever had with his father. The more he talked, the more he remembered. In reciting his list of injustices and rejections, he also told his father a whole history about himself that A. D. had not known.

Many of us have found that anger in a family situation usually overlies disillusioned love. Sometimes this doesn't seem possible. To the people involved, the anger may appear so monumental it is inconceivable that there is anything but bottomless rage. Yet, if it is all put into words without opposition, in time loving feelings will often surface.

Psychologists have learned that when anger is expressed against opposition, the anger seems to bounce back and be reabsorbed. But when anger is expressed without opposition, it largely dissipates. So it's easy to see that persuading whoever is angry at you to put those feelings into words without opposition is a fine way of getting rid of that person's anger, defusing the bomb, if you will.

It takes great self-control to allow— even encourage—someone to pour anger all over you. And there is a limit. An angry attack is encouraged; a venomous attack must be halted, usually by saying something to the effect of "You're going too far. That hurts too much." But that didn't happen in this case.

A. D. found the strength to sit there and not answer back. He did not defend himself, but simply listened and invited more. Some of what Alexander said made a kind of sense to A. D., and some of it was dead wrong. But he never interrupted, never disagreed, never argued, never explained himself, and certainly never pointed out where Alexander was wrong. If A. D. had defended himself, he would only have continued the war he was determined to stop.

Instead, A. D. said very little, being intent on listening and trying to understand. When Alexander finished, A. D. said he realized he had made a lot of mistakes and was sorry. The result was a cleansing and the end of the war.

By accepting his son's complaints without defending himself, A. D. was joining his son's resistance to acknowledging loving feelings for his father. How could Alexander love such a withholding father? By implicitly agreeing that Alexander could not be expected to love his father, A. D. made it possible for him to do so. Joining dissolves resistance.

After Alexander had finished his last complaint—to the surprise of them both—he was finally able to tell A. D. how glad he was that he had come to Los Angeles. Only then did A. D. tell his son of his effort to get help because of the importance of his son to him. To their mutual chagrin, they both fought tears.

A. D. still didn't understand his own incapacity for feelings, and when he tried to explain, his fumbling efforts were truly terrible. He did, however, manage not to criticize anymore, and his son loved him for that and for his effort. It was his father's determination to end the war and his struggle for emotional honesty that brought Alexander around.

By that time it was almost 4:00 in the morning and they went out together to an all-night diner for an early breakfast.

It was a wonderful conversation both for what it accomplished and for what it foreshadowed. A. D. and Alexander had ended their war and were negotiating an emotional peace. Each had needs to consider. There were limits to what A. D. could do. That meant there had to be limits on what Alexander could demand. But by talking—and talking and talking—the two men had arrived at the beginnings of a feeling relationship, the father–son relationship both of them had always wanted and neither of them had known how to have.

But there was another war in A. D. and Beth's family, the real reason Beth had urged A. D. to come with her into family therapy. It had to do with their younger son, Fletcher.

Beth had always doted on Fletcher. Alexander had been a "stress" baby, one of those babies for whom the world seemed a troublesome place for many months. Early on, Alexander gave Beth that "bad mother" feeling. She was an insecure new mother and felt deeply inadequate when he developed colic and again when he was put on a soybean formula because he couldn't digest her milk.

Fletcher, on the other hand, had been easy from the start, a "flow baby." Because he was born about the time that A. D. began to retreat back into his impersonal self, Beth had turned to her younger son for emotional sustenance.

For twenty years, Fletcher was her joy. He did well in school, was captain of this and president of that, a great, all-around kid. Even his adolescence wasn't so bad; he simply absented himself, staying in his room for the better part of two years—(copies of *Penthouse* under his mattress)—and then emerged with a deeper voice and the beginnings of a beard. Adults liked him, boys liked him, girls liked him.

Girls liked him too much, and that was when Beth began to truly suffer. She had accepted the loss of Alexander when he went off to college and later to music school, but the potential loss of Fletcher was too painful to even think about. (In order for her to keep Fletcher close, Beth had decided that he would go into his father's company.)

Trouble came as a dirty blonde, definitely on the skinny side, with a curious absence of social graces, and ambitions for Fletcher that did not include the family business. When Fletcher began "going" with Lisa, it was difficult for Beth to conceal her fear and her contempt. On one occasion, when Fletcher and Lisa broke up, Beth told Fletcher she was much relieved, that Lisa was far too "common" and he could do so much better.

The following week Fletcher and Lisa reconciled.

Beth, suspecting Fletcher had repeated her words to Lisa, became very anxious. Later, when Fletcher and Lisa began to talk about marriage, she became frantic. She tried to convince them they were too young, too inexperienced, and would regret an impulsive early marriage. They then informed her that Lisa was two months pregnant, and that ended the discussion.

Beth was horribly upset but made a conscientious effort to repair her relationship with her new daughter-in-law. She bought her maternity clothes ("So she won't look homeless!"), surprised her with casseroles ("This is Fletcher's favorite!"), and took a great deal of interest in the decoration of the small apartment that

Fletcher and Lisa had rented ("I had to bring you a sample of this fabric!").

For some reason Beth couldn't fathom, in spite of all her efforts, tension between the two women increased. By the time the baby was born ("Roger" after Lisa's father, and why not "Arthur" after A. D.?) Lisa seemed to be having difficulty speaking to her mother-in-law. She cried a lot or said she needed to be alone with her baby. Beth bought clothes for little Roger, and Lisa had hysterics. Then real trouble began.

Lisa had trouble nursing and said Beth made her so nervous her milk wouldn't come in. So Beth found herself forced to stay away, although she did talk to Lisa twice a day on the phone. That became difficult because she always seemed to catch Lisa in the middle of something and one of the signs of Lisa's lack of manners was her forgetfulness about calling back. Fletcher would drop by for visits, but Lisa and Roger usually stayed home. At Thanksgiving, they did all come to dinner, but Lisa had to leave right after eating. At Christmas, she and Fletcher and little Roger spent the better part of three days with her family.

Beth was now obsessing about Lisa. She awoke in the middle of the night talking to her rejecting daughter-in-law. A. D., who by this time had begun to come to terms with his own remoteness and wanted to be supportive of Beth, reached out to her, but his efforts were not enough. She could not shake her fury at being badly treated by Lisa.

In our offices, we speculated that Fletcher had chosen Lisa because she was needy like his mother and also because she would help him get away from his mother, which he had to do if he wasn't to end up spending his life as a little boy taking care of his mommy.

The question here was whether or not anything could be done. The answer, of course, was that something could be done provided Beth wanted something done. What was most fortunate for Beth and A. D. was that their problems with their children had driven them into treatment together because they needed to go through a maturational process—*together*. In that way, they could grow closer to each other, and their relationships with their children could be more rewarding to them both.

As we've already described, A. D. had made great progress with Alexander, but Beth was still struggling with Fletcher and Lisa. The crisis came soon enough when Lisa asked Beth if she would stop phoning so frequently. The ringing of the phone upset the baby. Beth was furious but what could she do?

The war was in full force, and Beth was losing her son and her grandson. It was a good time to reassess and give up the need to win the war. Unfortunately, Beth was so hurt and so angry that she couldn't find her way to that solution. A. D. tried to talk to her but she couldn't listen. Instead, she attacked, all guns blazing. She went to Fletcher and complained bitterly about Lisa's treatment of her. In turn, Lisa got an earful from Fletcher and called Beth. A good old-fashioned screaming ensued, with both women feeling misunderstood and assaulted—criticized and blamed, if you will, by the other.

Now they weren't speaking, which suited Lisa just fine and left Beth feeling miserable, furious, and abandoned. In the next few months, Lisa took every opportunity to insist that she and Fletcher spend holidays, birthdays, and other special occasions with *her* family. After all, they could hardly go to *his* family after the way Lisa had been treated.

A. D. and Beth saw Fletcher every ten days or so when he'd drop by during the evenings—and that was it.

The longer the standoff went on, the more Beth's upset increased. She ranted and raved, paced the living room floor like a restless lioness, and then began to cry and cry and cry.

Even in his remoteness, A. D. was able to understand that Beth's distress was a cry for help. He insisted she arrange for some individual therapy sessions to work on her difficulties with Lisa. Beth welcomed the opportunity, which was the most important part of all this. If she hadn't *wanted* help, she wouldn't have been able to get it.

As we had with A. D., we began by asking Beth what her goals were regarding Lisa.

Beth didn't know where to begin. Better manners? Less rudeness? More consideration? She'd certainly like to see more of her son and her grandson! All she knew was that she couldn't bear the present situation.

We asked her if she was saying that she wanted the war between her and her daughter-in-law to end? She thought for a long moment and then said she did, she really did.

When it became clear that Beth was willing to do anything to reach that goal—including losing the war—we suggested that she use the same tactics with Lisa that A. D. had used with Alexander. Beth listened to us, partly because she thought we were on her side, but mostly because she knew that A. D.'s relationship with Alexander had improved dramatically.

It still took many painful sessions before Beth was able to act on our suggestion. At one session, Beth would be willing to do anything; by the next session she'd decided she wanted Lisa crawling to her, begging for forgiveness. Even during her most rational moments, Beth still didn't feel she had the self-control to surrender to her daughter-in-law. Beth was too hurt not to express her own opinion, not to tell Lisa how very much pain she had inflicted with her rudeness and coldness. It was only after the same complaints had been repeated time after time and had lost much of their force that Beth was finally able to agree to try to get Lisa to express her side—without opposition.

Heart in her mouth, Beth phoned Lisa and said she wanted to come over and apologize and would Lisa allow her to do so? After some cautious negotiations, Lisa agreed. Beth suggested Lisa get a babysitter—whom Beth would pay—so they wouldn't be interrupted. Lisa brightened at that, clearly welcoming the idea of a little help with the baby.

Trying to keep her hands from trembling, Beth went over to Lisa's house and said she was glad to see her. She said it because it was true. She had hated being shut out of her son's home, and she was glad to be permitted to be there again. Beth had promised herself not to tell anything but the absolute truth because she knew Lisa would sense it if she lied. And lying, of course, was opposition.

After admiring little Roger briefly, Beth said she had come to apologize but didn't really know what she was apologizing for. She believed Lisa was very angry with her, possibly hurt, and perhaps disappointed, which suggested Beth had done something wrong. Beth didn't know what she had done wrong and asked Lisa to do her the kindness of telling her.

Lisa, of course, refused.

Beth persisted, and in time, tentatively at first, Lisa began to describe her side of what had happened. She began with incidents Beth had long forgotten but which still burned in Lisa's memory, incidents that had happened when she and Fletcher were first keeping company and Beth had given her the very distinct feeling that she wasn't "good enough" for Fletcher.

Beth was shocked because she knew it was true. She did have those feelings and had to admit to herself that she'd been willing, in some kind of arrogance, to allow Lisa to pick them up. When she accepted responsibility for those remarks without explanation, without defending herself, without opposition, Lisa began to feel free to tell her mother-in-law all the things that she had done.

Beth did a good job. She listened and introduced her own agenda only once, when she asked for a cup of coffee. Lisa seemed glad to get it. As they were resuming, Fletcher came in and was surprised to find his mother there. The two women explained they were having a private conversation and asked him to allow them to continue. He left, and Lisa resumed her litany of the condescensions, the slights, the rudenesses that she felt she had experienced at the hands of her mother-in-law.

Beth had rehearsed the scene with us and with A. D., and she knew her role was to help Lisa put her anger into words. So rather than defend herself, rather than offer the slightest opposition, Beth kept asking Lisa to go on, tell her more. And Lisa did. As she did so, it became surprisingly clear that she had been terribly intimidated by Beth and A. D., had felt absolutely unworthy of Fletcher, and felt horribly guilty that she had "trapped" him into marriage by getting pregnant. Everything her mother-in-law had done had exacerbated Lisa's self-doubts, and in time, even being in the same room with Beth was more pain than Lisa could endure.

As Lisa went on, Beth realized that a case could be made for the argument that *she* had been the one with bad manners. *She* had been the one who had treated Lisa rudely. *She* had been the one who was cold. When Lisa finished, Beth said simply that she wondered how a simple apology for all that she had done wrong could possibly be enough? What she could do to atone for how badly she had treated Lisa?

As often happens when real home truths are shared without opposition, Lisa then cried and so did Beth. For the first time in her life, Beth had the impulse to give Lisa a genuine hug. She asked permission and did so. Then they phoned A. D. and asked him to come over for an impromptu dinner.

A. D. and Beth did a remarkable job of stopping the wars within the family, and their life is now much closer to what they had hoped for. Once Beth had made peace with her daughter-in-law, she no longer felt the need for treatment. A. D., on the other hand, has remained in individual therapy and believes that it is increasing his ability "to feel."

Family wars are the source of infinite pain. The only way to stop a family war is to give up being right. Victory is built on listening, not telling, on apology, not on "I told you so" or "The trouble with you is . . ."

4

The Tragedy of Addiction:
Alcohol and Drugs

The only nice thing about addiction is that it has no prejudice; it does not discriminate on the basis of race, color, creed, gender-identification, class, economic power, quality of mind or spirit, or general niceness or meanness. Everyone is welcome. And it is a brute. Addiction to alcohol or drugs is an enemy that no single person, no single family, no single doctor, no single priest can fight alone. It is the biggest problem a family will face besides a terminal illness, and many times, alcohol or drug addiction is a terminal illness.

Alcohol and drug addiction are cunning, baffling, and astonishingly persistent and powerful. If you are a parent with an addicted child, we wish we could reach out from these pages and put our arms around you. Since we cannot, at least we can help you fight the hardest battle in which you will ever be engaged.

If you have reached the point where you have recognized that your child is an addict of alcohol or drugs (eating disorders, gambling, and compulsive working are in the next chapter)—and it is a terrible moment of realization—then you have taken the first vital step and that first step is perhaps the single most important thing that you will do in fighting addiction. While recognition may seem to you nothing but an awful onset of pain, you have begun a long pilgrimage and, as the Chinese have written, "a journey of a thousand miles begins with a single step." Your pilgrimage starts with the step of recognition.

Denial

What usually stands in the way of recognition is an unconscious need to avoid pain. The mind often simply declines to recognize what hurts too much. Psychologists call this mechanism "denial" and we all do it. The difficulty is that denial paralyzes. It is universal among addicts and among the family members of addicts. If there is one commonality among alcoholics, drug users, and their family members and friends, it is that so many of them deny the existence of any addiction.

How do you know your child is addicted? One commonsense answer is that if alcohol or drugs has *a significant negative impact* on your child's life, then you have to know you're dealing with addiction. If a life-style is being modified to satisfy the needs of the substance, or personal relationships are being damaged, or jobs lost, or debt incurred, or there is the risk of prison, those are all tip-offs.

When you've gone through the agony of assessment, wanting not to believe what is obvious to many others, and you've been forced to the realization that your child is indeed, tragically, addicted, you have faced the abyss. Your next step is quite simple.

Do Nothing

Actually, it was a school psychologist many years ago who made a seminal recommendation to a parent-teacher association. "The longer I have worked with troubled children the more convinced I have become that in almost every crisis the best answer is do nothing."

It is still a good answer when a problem is first identified. And above all . . .

Don't Talk to Your Child

When a parent realizes a child is in danger, there is an immediate impulse to rush in and rescue. But there are two primary reasons for not making that attempt. The first is that you almost certainly don't know enough about addiction in general and your child's addiction in particular (when it happened, why it happened, how it happened, where it is headed, and to whom your child can turn).

The second reason is that, in the urge to rescue, it is virtually impossible not to give unsolicited advice and/or to criticize. If you say, "We're so worried about you" what is the message? What does your child hear? How about "You're making us worry" or "You're making us worry again, the way you did when you were a kid" or "You've really done it, this time." Criticism and blaming will only make matters worse.

So, until you've made yourself knowledgeable and until you've discovered your own role in your child's addiction and learned to control your impulses to blame or criticize, it is extremely unlikely that you can be helpful. It is highly probable that instead you will be counterproductive, producing an argument instead of a healing, an insult instead of a helping hand.

In the moment of recognition, it is vitally important that you focus on yourself rather than on your child. At this stage we are primarily concerned *with you*. In fact, this chapter is about you and what you can do and only marginally about your child.

Perhaps the most painful event that follows the realization that your child is an addict is to hear the words "addiction is a family problem." You may have a family consisting of the most wonderful people in the world, the most loving, the brightest, the strongest, the most generous, a family in which all the members love each other and want nothing but the best for one another, but unfortunately the overall system created by all of you together is toxic, damaging, and unmanageable.

Addiction is a disease with its roots in the family—which includes the genetic pool and the family. It is influenced by both nature and nurture. Addiction is often found in several generations of a family, telling you that there is a vulnerability to addiction in your family. Then there is *nurture*, which includes not only family members but societal stressors—forced separations, financial troubles, and many others. Stress comes in an infinite number of forms.

Blaming and Criticism Are Counterproductive

Realizing that the situation is far more complicated than father-is-to-blame or mother-is-to-blame or we-are-both-to-blame, there is an immediate need to stop all blaming and criticism of yourselves. Blaming and criticism of you or the addict will only make things worse. If there is one lesson psychologists have learned in this situation it is that blaming yourself or your child or society is counterproductive. So what do you do instead?

Know Your Enemy

Begin now, quite simply, by educating yourself about the problem with which you are dealing. You may want to read, talk to friends, talk to doctors or priests, talk to therapists.

Join a Support Group

By far the best way to get to know your enemy is to join a support group made up of people like yourselves who have been wrestling with the same problem. Many of the support groups we recommend are free and all are powerful. Do not pass go. Do not collect two hundred dollars. Find a support group for you.

This is what's called a sticking place. It is one thing to recognize that your child is an addict; it is quite another to publicly acknowledge it. Most people find the idea of joining a support group a terribly painful thought indeed. Could you join a support group anyway if it was in your own best interest and in the best interest of your child? The fear of admitting in front of strangers that you are the parent of an addict can fill you with apprehension. You may expect to be criticized or humiliated or shamed. The reality, of course, will be quite different. Parents joining a support group will find that they are welcomed generously and will experience great relief once they have managed to take the difficult first step of going to that first meeting.

What group should you join? Believe it or not there are many choices. The answer is to begin asking around—in person or on the phone—to find which groups have chapters in your area and what services they provide. You can get a great deal of information simply by making a call to any public or private alcohol or drug treatment facility. In some cities, you can find a chapter of Co-Dependents Anonymous. But by far the largest and most

accessible source of help is Alcoholics Anonymous, an organization which has been an inspiration to people suffering from many
kinds of addiction and from which there have been numerous
spin-offs.

Right now your addicted child has available:

Alcoholics Anonymous
Narcotics Anonymous

These are self-help groups for addicts. One of the principles
that guides them is the idea that a recovering addict is the best
person to try to help an active addict.

But for each of these groups there is a second group that is *not*
for addicts but for *the families and friends* of addicts, and these
groups operate on the theory that the parents and friends of
addicts are the best people to try to help the parents and friends of
addicts. These groups for parents are called:

Al-Anon
Narc-Anon, sometimes Nar-Anon.

Parents who have come to the realization that a child is an
addict can get in touch with Alcoholics Anonymous and learn
how to contact the nearest Al-Anon or Narc-Anon group.

There is apt to be resistance to that suggestion.

Not so long ago the authors of this book had a call from an old
friend. Martha's first husband was alcoholic, and they were
divorced. Recently she had realized that her second husband was
also alcoholic, and their marriage was in difficulty. Martha had
also known for some time that one of her daughters was abusing
alcohol.

Now she called us in real agony because she had just learned
that her oldest and most-adored son was almost surely addicted to

cocaine. She cried and cried, then asked what she should do.

We told her to find the nearest branch of Narc-Anon. She brushed that suggestion aside. She wanted a book. She wanted to read something. She wanted to find out what advice to give her son. (After all, it was *his* problem.) We suggested that she call Alcoholics Anonymous and talk to them about possible reading. She brushed that suggestion aside. She didn't want to talk to AA. She wanted some psychology.

To Martha the idea that addiction is a family problem and that every family member, including her, might be involved, is too painful to tolerate. Repeated recommendations of Narc-Anon were rebuffed.

It was evident that while Martha was calling for help, she didn't really want help. She simply wanted the feeling that she was doing everything she could, which, of course, she was not.

The Enabler

Martha is a classic enabler. Despite the fact that she has been married to two alcoholic husbands and is mother to two substance-abusing children, she cannot even contemplate the idea that she might be involved in any way.

An enabler is someone who helps the addict stay addicted. An enabler will do wonderful things for the addict—like calling the job and making an excuse when the addict is too drunk to go in to work—or putting money in a bank account to cover a bouncing check—or giving money to the addict that will ultimately be used to support the addiction—or making excuses in the family for the failure of the addict to attend a family function.

An enabler will help the addict stay addicted and, since addiction is a progressive disease, will actually help the addict get worse.

Martha is a classic enabler. Nothing would persuade her that reading a psychological study of drug addiction wasn't the appropriate step for her to take and that calling Narc-Anon was. She was convinced that it was *her son's problem*, and she wanted to find out what *he* should do about it. The idea that it was also *her* problem and that *her* first step should be to deal with *herself* was simply unacceptable.

Several months have passed since her phone call to us. Martha's son is more seriously addicted, and Martha is still reading psychological studies. Everything she reads informs her that addiction is a family disease—and somehow those words never register.

Alcoholics Anonymous

Whatever the addiction, Al-Anon (for the family and friends of alcoholics) or Narc-Anon (for the family and friends of drug-users) is there to help. But it all began with Alcoholics Anonymous.

What is Alcoholics Anonymous?

Very simply, it is a self-help group. In the 1920s, a group of men in Akron, Ohio, realizing they were unable to control their drinking, came to the conclusion that alcoholism was not a sin but a physiological, emotional, and spiritual *disease*. It also became clear to them that they could not get sober alone but that if they helped each other they might. Their guiding premise was that each of them had failed to conquer the disease by himself, and each of them had to have the help of a power greater than himself if he was to recover.

Together that little group of men developed a 12-Step Program that has gone on to help millions. All over the United States—all over the world for that matter—there are spin-offs from that original 12-Step Program. Alcohol and drug programs, eating disorder programs, compulsive behavior programs, hospitals, churches, and therapists have found that the 12-Step Programs are ultimately the only real weapons we have in the fight against addiction. And it all began with Alcoholics Anonymous—AA.

One word of caution: Not everyone is able to benefit from these programs. In fact, many people are so in the grips of the addiction that they cannot stay within the twelve steps. But AA still remains the very best hope we have.

Let us take a very quick look at the AA program, as it is the basis of so many other self-help programs, whether the problem is alcohol or drugs. And it is always the place to begin.

The 12-Step Program

Step 1 . . . is to say "We admit it. We are powerless over alcohol. Our lives have become unmanageable."

For the parents of an addict that means to accept the idea that they are powerless over the addict and the addiction, and that their lives are consequently unmanageable.

Step 2 . . . is to say "We have come to believe that a Power greater than ourselves can restore us to health."

For some parents this will mean God; for others it may simply mean the Power of The Group. Whatever higher power is chosen will do.

Step 3 . . . is to say "We have made a decision to turn our will and our lives over to the care of God as we understand him."

One of the brilliant aspects of AA is that it is not part of any organized religion. It does not tell people what to believe but strongly suggests—AA never insists, only suggests—that people must have help from a power greater than themselves if they are to beat the addiction. This is an idea especially valuable to parents.

The first three steps of AA ask parents to *truly* acknowledge that they cannot deal with the problem on their own and would benefit from help from a higher power.

Step 4 . . . is to say "We have made a searching and fearless moral inventory of ourselves."

In order to change the family dynamics, parents need to get rid of the debris of the past—guilt and self-blaming are the principal culprits. Exploring their own piece of the puzzle, with the support of the others in the group, is not as painful as it might seem from the outside. It is an experience in which the others have shared and for which there is understanding and compassion.

Step 5 . . . is to say "We have admitted to God, to ourselves, and to another human being *the exact nature of our wrongs."*

The fifth step is brilliant and pivotal. When each parent is ready he or she picks a very reliable, safe person—a minister, a therapist, or a highly trusted fellow member of the group, to be a "sponsor" and admits the findings of the "fearless moral inventory." Putting the debris of the past into words gets rid of it. AA *takes the position that they look at the past but do not dwell on it.*

Step 6 . . . is to say "We are entirely ready to have God [or the individual's Higher Power] remove all these defects of character."

Step 7 . . . is to "humbly ask Him to remove our short comings."

Step 8 . . . is to "make a list of all persons we have harmed and become willing to make amends to them all."

Step 9 . . . is to "make amends to such people wherever possible, except when to do so would injure them or others."

These steps—getting rid of guilt, repairing relationships, changing our ways of dealing with others—brings an ineffable peace.

The last three steps simply aim to continue what has already been done.

Step 10 . . . is to "continue to take personal inventory and when we are wrong admit it promptly."

Step 11 . . . is to "seek through prayer and meditation to improve our conscious contact with God as we understand him, praying for knowledge of His will for us and the power to carry that forth."

AA's reliance on a divine power is comforting to many. But for others the heavy attention to God is troublesome. Some members of AA resolve that problem by substituting "the Power of The

Group" whenever the word "God" is used.

The final step is the payoff. It is the reward that enhances the meaning of the program.

Step 12 . . . is to say "that having had a spiritual awakening as a result of these steps we will carry the message to others who still suffer."

One of the reasons that 12-Step groups are so welcoming is that some members are working on their twelfth Step.

We have taken the time in this chapter to describe the AA 12-Step Program at length not only because the program is so vital but because laying it out in detail reinforces the time and effort required to deal successfully with addiction. Addiction is never an easy problem; there is no "quick fix"; but with intelligence and effort there is always hope.

It is important to note that a 12-Step Program involves a fundamental change in life-style. Such a transformation not only takes time to accomplish, but most successful members remain within the program indefinitely in order to guard against a "slip."

Out of the Problem and Into the Solution

In the beginning, a 12-Step Program is apt to overwhelm parents with information. But before very long you will have consulted with other parents—who have been dealing with the same problem that you're facing—and you will feel relieved and informed.

Al-Anon and Narc-Anon help parents identify their family's roles and their own roles in the addiction and provide the support and the practical suggestions parents need to help them get their addicted children into treatment. The hardest lesson parents have to learn is not to bail out the addict, not to fix, not to advise, not to do any of the things that are enabling to the addict.

Talk to Your Child

Now it is time to talk to your child. You have resisted the impulse to rush in to rescue. You have obtained a support group for yourself. You have spoken with knowledgeable people who have been through the horror in which you find yourself. You intend to stay in the program as a source of ongoing help *because you will need ongoing help*. You have learned a great deal about addiction, enablers, and the great variety of therapeutic resources that are available. You're aware of the dangers inherent in blaming your child or yourself for the problem with which you're all involved. You're ready now.

Tough Love

The concept of "tough love" springs from the idea that there is the love that heals and the love that cripples. Beth's love for Fletcher (see chapter 3) was rooted in her own neediness and was not caring for him. That's the kind of love that cripples. In the same way, Martha's love for her two husbands and for her children was rooted in *her* own neediness and was not rooted in caring for them. Her approach to helping her youngest son is another example of the kind of love that cripples. The love of an "enabler" like Martha helps a situation worse. This book is based on the premise that change is always possible. Simply because there is a history of enabling does not mean that enabling has to continue. Let's look at another case.

Doris was the widowed mother of Robert, twenty-five, and living at home. A businesswoman and a deeply caring mother, Doris had made Robert the mainstay of her life since his father's death. She knew he had experimented with marijuana in high school and that in college snorting cocaine was a recreation of choice. She never spoke to him about his early drug use. She expected that Robert would sample and move on. He didn't.

Robert never could identify any work in which he was interested, but he could identify his drug of choice: cocaine. After college he had a series of jobs, but most of his interest was in seeing his friends. Actually, his only real interest was in getting high. It wasn't until things began disappearing from the house that Doris started to suspect how serious Robert's problem was, but the idea that he was actually stealing from her still seemed incomprehensible. She thought about it and then, as she explained, "I put it out of my mind."

Doris was the master of denial. She was also a classic enabler because she was allowing Robert to steal her things and sell them in order to sustain his habit. It wasn't until months later, when she found him going out the door with a clock under his coat, that she acknowledged the depth of the problem to herself. Denial was no longer possible.

By this time Robert had been using mood-changing substances for eight years. Doris now made the mistake of rushing in to rescue by trying to talk to him and show him the error of his ways. He abruptly moved out of the house.

Now Doris had heard of the concept of "tough love." But she didn't really understand it. She didn't really understand much about substance abuse, either. She thought that if she washed her hands of Robert, gave him no money—unless he was absolutely desperate—that he would be forced to mend his ways.

Robert came back to her house one day when she was out and stole her dining room table, which, of course, he sold for money with which to buy drugs.

A terrified Doris—an angry Doris, actually—found herself not knowing what to do. This highly intelligent, highly capable businesswoman was awash in indecision. She changed the locks on the house and that was all. Robert stayed away for several weeks. Doris worried. And worried. So actually there was some relief when she awakened one morning to find him, cold, dirty, and hungry, sleeping on her doorstep. He swore he would never use drugs again if she would take him in.

But there was something about that promise that goaded Doris into action. She took Robert back into the house, but she knew he was lying to her. There was something about being lied to that convinced her she was in over her head and had to get help.

Doris went to Narc-Anon until she was ready to talk to Robert. Then she began a series of conversations with him—to no avail. She told him he would have to move out of the house unless he entered a rehabilitation program. He swore to her he didn't need rehab, that he was clean and would remain clean. Doris, who still had something of the enabler in her and who, in spite of being informed, didn't want to accept the fact that her son was truly addicted, gave him the benefit of the doubt. On occasion she also gave him small sums of money—to buy wedding presents for his friends or business gifts. He bought drugs, of course.

The crisis came when she found a coke pipe in the pocket of a pair of blue jeans she was about to wash. She knew then the reality of her troubles. It was time for tough love. When Robert came home she informed him of her decision.

"Robert, either you're flying with me tonight to Minnesota or you can pack your things and leave."

"Minnesota?"

"There's a rehab center there that's highly recommended. They have a place for you—provided we're there in the morning."

"Mom! It's a blizzard out!"

"You don't have a third choice. It's come with me tonight or go out the door."

"How could I go out the door? I haven't any money."

"That's not my problem."

"MOM!"

"If you argue with me, I'll call your uncle and have you put out. And the locks will be changed again tomorrow."

"But what would I do? Where would I go?"

"As I said, that's not my problem."

The initial visit to Minnesota was successful. Doris left Robert there for thirty days. When he returned to New York he entered a 12-Step Group and went into therapy. So far the results seem to have been positive.

Doris had learned how deep her denial had been about Robert's addiction and that she had been part of the problem. She began to work on herself. She realized the first message the twelve steps give us—that she was powerless over Robert and his cocaine. That all she had power over was herself.

Doris worked the twelve steps in Al-Anon and found a whole new way of looking at the world and a new way of living. She found a sponsor who is now her closest friend. She took care of herself since that was the only thing she could do. Fortunately Robert's story was a happy one.

Many addiction stories are not so happy. All we can do is try. But—and it's a big BUT—knowledge and the right kind of love can move mountains. Many addicts *do* get help; many addicts *do* go on to live productive and rewarding lives. And many parents of addicts come to be at peace with themselves.

For more on addiction please go on to the next chapter.

5

The Tragedy of Other Addictions:
Eating Disorders

One of the most important things we can share with you about eating disorders is that there is a vast amount of knowledge we don't have about them. Surprised? The common wisdom is that if people eat the right amount of food and expend the right amount of energy, they will be at the proper body weight for good health. This is by no means the whole story. We know that societal, genetic, environmental, psychological, and physiological factors all play a part. By no means do we have all the information on what makes people fat or thin—obese, bulimic, or anorexic.

On the other hand, many of us think we know a great deal. We think we have the answers. This leads to terrible prejudice against those who suffer from eating disorders and their families. Not quite enough knowledge is as dangerous as too little. As things are, a fat person is looked on by society as an out of control glutton whose opinions, needs, and desires don't matter that much. Fat people comprise the only group of which it is still "politically correct" to make fun. They earn less money, have worse jobs, enjoy less social acceptance, and have a harder time finding mates. And, of course, they themselves often buy into the attitudes that underlie their punishment. "Since everybody thinks people like me are so rotten, and social slights hurt so much, there's no point in going out; I might as well stay home and eat."

It is no wonder, therefore, that so many of our young women become bulimic and anorexic. They know the price of fat is all of the above. They will do anything and give up anything to be thin. The bulimic will destroy her esophagus—at the least—and the anorexic will diet to the point that her body's mechanisms are so thrown out of kilter that she becomes literally insane—which is to say she loses all sense of reality about her body. Even when an anorexic young woman is a wraith, she still truly believes she is fat. She takes on some of the characteristics of schizophrenia and obsessive-compulsive disorder. What begins as a diet becomes an ever-widening mania of exercise and obsession with food to the exclusion of all other interests. If unchecked, the young woman will continue to lose weight until she starves to death.

When we don't know the answers, we blame the victim. We can look back at other diseases that caused their victims social ostracism and see how this was lifted once the disease had a cure. In the 1920s, rickets was looked on with distaste and thought to be a disease of poverty, neglect, and the lower classes. As soon as it was found to be caused by a vitamin D deficiency, the stigma of the disease was lifted. Who doesn't love success? The doctors were thrilled to have an answer, and rickets is no longer a source of shame. Consider autism. Mothers were told it was because of a lack of warmth and good mothering that their child was autistic. Many fine and caring parents were devastated by this condemnation from the experts. Autism is now understood not to be caused by the way the infant is parented.

For parents who are afflicted with eating disorders—or who have children suffering from them—it is important to get rid of all blame and shame. This is difficult because we are all slaves to the values of our society. If we don't fit into the norm, we attack ourselves. The first line of defense is getting rid of the prejudice against ourselves and our children. The second is to understand what is known of the problem. The third is to find others similarly affected and work with them at finding solutions. Dr. Carol Brod[1] says one should join an eating disorder group—not necessarily to lose a hundred pounds but to keep up with what's going on in the field and to get support and esteem from others with the same affliction.

Mostly Affects Women

In this chapter we are going to refer to the child as "she" since women suffer from eating disorders more than men and in different ways. Let us say, though, that the devastation of being overweight is just as destructive to men as to women. Fat men suffer from ridicule, disrespect in the market place, worse jobs, and also have trouble finding mates. What is written in this chapter applies to them, although they do not usually suffer from anorexia and bulimia as frequently as women.

So Your Kid Comes Home Different from When She Left

What should a parent do if a child comes home after college or a stint away from home "morbidly fat" or "morbidly thin?" Note the word *morbid*. An ugly word. It means "deathly," and it is used medically as a diagnostic description. One out of three Americans are overweight. The statistics for the obese are out of sight and

1. Of the Center for Modern Psychoanalytic Studies, NYC; see Acknowledgments

steadily rising. We are becoming a morbidly fat nation, and a look at television and the media could lead us to believe we are also becoming a morbidly anxious one when it comes to issues of food and weight. As I write this chapter, I have the television on in the background. Every twenty minutes, a commercial sells me a fat remedy, and every other twenty minutes, a Big Mac with double fries. I take a break and look at a magazine. Most of the articles are about diet and exercise, and most of the ads are cake recipes—real or low fat—chocolate pours out at me in swirls. It isn't just your kid that has an eating disorder, it's the whole country.

Probably the onset of your kid's eating disorder will have started long before adulthood, but it might have been exacerbated by the conflicts brought on by her forays into adulthood. Maybe you tried to control her life when she was small in order to save her from unhappiness. Now she is an adult and a big emotional shift is due. You can't control an adult child. How much responsibility do you now have for your child? How much influence? Is "control" of anybody a good idea in the first place? One thing we can say about the emotional dynamic of eating disorders: they are all about control—of feelings, of tension, of the world, and of you, the parents.

Let's begin now with anorexia.

Anorexia

There are all degrees of treatment. At the very worst, if your kid is starving to death—say she's five seven and weighs seventy-nine pounds—you get her into a hospital even if you have to call 911. She will honestly believe she's simply fine and simply trying to lose her ugly fat. Yes, at seventy-nine pounds she will still be convinced that she is fat and will be angry that you don't agree with her. Well, if she thought it was fine to walk in front of a truck, you'd pull her off the road and worry about her adult autonomy later. When death by starvation threatens, you get her help ASAP. In the hospital, they will stabilize her body and get some nutrients into her. Afterward she needs to be treated with a multiteam approach, which is the best plan we have so far to handle all degrees of anorexia, bulimia, and morbid obesity. She will need an internist to monitor her medical problems. She will need a nutritionist in whom she has absolute confidence to work with her to help make a diet plan that she likes AND trusts will not make her obese. She will need a psychiatrist to determine if she needs psychotropic drugs and, if she does, to administer them. This is not a job for an internist. Drug therapy is a specialized science these days and needs an expert. Most importantly, she needs a therapist to help her with her body image, give her support, and help her find out why she is starving herself. Every patient is an individual with a different dynamic; every patient's condition is serious and needs a multifaceted approach.

You and your daughter can get help—hopefully when you first encounter this problem—by calling the Anorexia Hot Line (1-800-736-3739) or any one of the various local organizations specializing in anorexia. You will find them in your local phone book. Remember that parents need help, too. For heaven sake, don't feel bad about it. Parents sometimes think they should do everything for their child themselves. That is as nonsensical as someone in our society saying they can't eat any food they haven't grown in their own back yard from scratch. We have many services and aids in our society. Let's use them.

What Do We Parents Do After the Initial Crisis?

Our kid is an adult. We do not have control of her life, her actions, her belief system. We cannot make an adult child do anything. Nevertheless, we are still parents. What is our job in the face of eating disorders? The paradox in that is that we never desert our child; we stand by her, we provide nurturing life enhancing support, but above all once the crisis of life and death is over, *we do nothing!*

That sounds like some daffy Zen koan, but that's the prescription. Before taking any action we study the situation. We try to understand what has happened so we can work through any mistakes we may have made that have contributed to the problem. We do this without blame and shame. Our thinking should be about our child and how we can help, not about ourselves as a parent who has a sick kid. We, as moms of kids with eating disorders, probably fall into one of the following categories:

1. We may be a naturally thin person endowed with a good metabolism who simply has no issue about food. How, when this is the case, can we understand a daughter whose fat genes and relation to food and eating are so very different from our own?

2. We might be a normal weight mom who looks dandy but who suffers from an underlying hysteria about food. We are always dieting, throwing up, frantically exercising, and worrying about every calorie and fat gram we ingest. Our families may or may not talk about this. All we know is, our daughter is acting out our problem.

3. We are fat ourselves but don't have a big issue about it. We may go on diets every once in a while and that's the sum of it. We'd like to be a size six, but meanwhile, life goes on and we're fairly okay. Our daughter in her separation and rebellion may be dieting so she will not be like us.

4. We may be a yo-yo dieter who is always going for either feast or famine. We are always dieting and then gorging for a treat because we've been so good. Like mothers 2 (above), we've probably put our kids into a double bind about food. On one

hand, we say diet and on the other, eat. We're like the mom who diets her seven-year-old on Slim Fast and then gives her a fudge sundae for being brave at the dentist.

Now, as for Dad. A daughter may want to live up to his expectations. A dad who is a wonderful father may accidentally be seductive without meaning to be by expressing his pride in how his daughter is developing as a woman and perhaps in how pretty she is. The daughter may be frightened by this—on an unconscious level—as her own sexuality begins to bud. Some anorexics are emotionally delayed in their emotional lives and turn to obsessive dieting to avoid having to deal with their sexuality and other grown-up responsibilities and tasks. This is often very hard to see because the young woman may be a high achiever with great intellectual gifts that make us think she is more mature than she is.

Why do we care about the above? As we've said, intellectual understanding is rarely of any help. These are emotional problems that require emotional solutions. And we're at the here and now. Our kid has a big problem. Before we can help, we need some help for ourselves. We parented as we were parented. Some of it was terrific and some wasn't. We need some TLC, some extra support, before we can help. A therapist is usually our best bet. If one is not available, we need a buddy. See chapter 8. We need the support of friends and family—that is the support of those who love us and love our child. We do not need anybody who wants to tell us what's wrong with us and our child and what we should do "for our own good." Haven't you noticed that whenever something was given to us for our own good it was unpleasant? Right now we need people who listen, who care, and who don't have any personal agendas about how we ought to be. And so does our kid.

Here's what we mean by doing nothing. We might ask our daughter if she would like to talk about her eating problem. If she says no, we say no more. If she does want to talk about it, we listen. We don't fix, jump in with suggestions. If she is angry with us and full of spleen about what we did or did not do that caused her problem when she was a child, we don't defend ourselves. We don't say "we did the best we could"; instead, we take responsibility for what we may not have handled well. We may share our own problem and admit that it may have contributed to hers and that we know more now than we did then. In other words, we respect her feelings as well as our own. We might then ask if there is anything she would like us to do to help, in the here and now. If she says no, we don't volunteer. If she has requests that we can meet, we meet them. We do just what she asks, no more, no less.

Sometimes the issues around control push our buttons. If our anorexic daughter or obese dieting daughter comes home and takes over our refrigerator with barrels of turnips and odd foods, we may have an impulse to battle for control of the kitchen. Control is often one of the most important issues underlying eating problems. The battle for the kitchen is a battle that should not be fought. One mother we know simply rented an extra refrigerator for her daughter's diet food and said, "Darling, this is for your stuff. We have dinner every night at six. We love to have you. You can eat our food or cook your own. You can eat with us or not as you please. You know our menus."

With eating disorders, the best thing we can do to win our daughter's health, is to lose the war of control. And fast.

Instead, we can focus on what we love about our daughter. We can work to find joy with her in activities we both enjoy. Put the food topic in mothballs. Think what we would say and do with her if she had no problem. Do the two of you enjoy buying clothes together? Then go shopping. Get her clothes if that's what she wants. You both like movies? Indulge. What besides eating and drinking does your family enjoy? Do it. Remember, your daughter is going through "nobody-tells-me-what-to-do; the-forces-of-the-world-particularly-you-Mom-and-Dad-are-trying-to-control-me-and-I-will-die-before-I-let-you." If your family likes exercise, go swimming, riding, a hike, a trip, anything that is enjoyable. Don't try to set up a vollcyball game through grilled teeth if all of you hate it. Maybe walks to another part of the city to try some new activity might be fun. Whatever, do something that brings joy. Play Scrabble if nothing else. Eat out if you all enjoy it. Just don't let the food be the issue. Let being together be the fun. And don't comment on what your daughter does or doesn't eat. If she's brought a thermos full of liquid diet glop get the waiter to bring her a nice glass. Abandon food as a topic or an issue.

Most importantly, do not vent your feelings about your daughter's food problem to her. Let her know you truly do think it's her business, not yours.

So how do we manage not to burst into tears when she looks like she has come from a concentration camp or has been blown up like a helium balloon? How do we handle our own pain at seeing our daughter suffer? We have to stay more mature because that's our job as parents. We are not her friend, buddy, or girl-friend; we're her parents. We gave her life and did the best we could in raising her. Now, adult that she is, she still needs us. She still needs us to be there like a big sturdy wall that doesn't crumble when she throws herself against it. She needs our recognition of her adult status and our recognition that she, not us, is in charge of her life. When we want to pick her up and fix her problems as we did when she was little, we cannot. We must accord her the respect and dignity and courtesy we would extend to any adult of our acquaintance. If we wouldn't say to our boss's wife "ohmygod how fat/thin you've gotten" and burst into tears, we don't say it to our daughter. And we never burst into tears. We cannot reiterate enough that our daughter's eating problem is about *her*, not about us—parents who have a kid with an eating problem. No, as parents we have to forego that satisfaction.

We have to release our tensions and feelings to someone else. We go to a therapist or a buddy to cry, to let it all out about how terrible and inadequate we feel because our child is in so much pain. We vent all our feelings about how bad we feel because our daughter is not fitting into the norm of *our* world. We admit all the painful, petty, and grim feelings we have. We admit our anger at having to cope with the problem. We cry, gnash our teeth, and scream if need be.

Then, when we've got it all out, we may want to look at our own lives. What do we need to add to them? What do we need to let go? Maybe we need to work through our own eating problems, addictions, and other roadblocks to well-being. Maybe we need to change some of our values and thinking. We must to learn to respect our daughter's thinking and life choices—even if they differ from our own or even if initially we hate some of them. Before we can be therapeutic for our daughter, we have to take care of ourselves. As the kids say, we gotta "get a life." And we need to obey the old adage, "Happy parents make happy children." The best thing we can do for our children is to be happy ourselves, solving or at least coming to terms with our own strengths and weaknesses. For those with eating disorders and those who have children with eating disorders, the biggest thing to remember is that they are not cured by will power.

What We Can Do Specifically

When our daughter directly asks for treatment, we can help her obtain it. Financially. If that's impossible, we can help her find a clinic that will treat her. We cannot treat her ourselves because we are part of the problem. The solution has to come from her and her health providers. All we can do is stay available if she needs us. We don't run off to Europe when she is dangerously thin or crying that she can't stop bingeing and/or throwing up. A parent needs always to be available, even if imperfect. It's a very hard job being a do-nothing available parent. Keep in mind the old adage,

"They also serve who only stand and wait." When our child is born we start saying good-bye with the first hello. All through their lives we say increasingly say bigger good-byes. Sometimes it hurts incredibly. We feel empty, bereft at first, when we give up owning and controlling the child of our very flesh. We have to form a new relationship based on mutual respect, trust, and difference. We have to say a new "hello." To a new person. To our adult daughter who is always our daughter but no longer our child.

Obesity and How One of These Authors Deals

Being fat in America takes more courage than Joan of Arc. I know. I am fat. Did you think the authors of this book were some paragons? No. We, like everyone else, have areas of malfunction, problems we haven't solved but to which we have had to adjust and find accommodation. In this chapter, we add to the dilemma of eating disorders and other addictions not only how we as parents can help our so afflicted adult children but also some thoughts on how we as parents can deal with problems we haven't been able to solve ourselves vis-à-vis our children. But first, let's take a detour into what we might laughingly call the Genesis of Addiction. For the apple in the following story substitute food, drugs, drink, compulsive sexualizing, compulsive working, any activity undertaken to avoid feelings.

The First Eating Disorder

Eating disorders are as old as humanity. The first was Eve's. She ate the forbidden apple. We might ask why. She says she was tempted by the snake. Well, that's what we're told, but how, we might ask, could she be she tempted when she lived in paradise? What could possibly be missing from her life in lovely Eden to made her even consider the snake's offer? She wanted knowledge? Ridiculous! She didn't even know what knowledge was. Could it be that it was because Adam was asleep and consequently not available to receive the love, food, and companionship that was the very purpose of her existence? After all, she had been created from a paltry rib of Adam's solely to be his helpmate. But when he was asleep, when he wasn't there, how could she provide for him? And if she couldn't provide for him, how could she exist?

Being lonely without Adam, Eve must have felt as if she were dying. She must have felt like one big hole of emptiness, that she was going to be swept away into the "no being" from which she and Adam came. So naturally, such feelings being unbearable, she grabbed for the apple when the snake offered. Knowledge, schmowledge. Anything to beat down the feelings of not existing, and the guilt of causing Adam to not be if she were not. Of course she also lost her and Adam's innocence and forever after had to deal with the terrible knowledge that she was separate from Adam, that she had feelings, wishes, angers, and longings separate from his. This produced the first guilt because she knew she was supposed to exist just for Adam's feelings, wishes, angers, and longings and not her own.

And it was no picnic for Adam either. Because he was doing something besides looking after Eve, i.e., sleeping, he was going to have to work, gleaning from the hard earth his and Eve's livelihood by the sweat of his brow. Since Eve had succumbed to existential angst without Adam, she was going to have to suffer in childbirth. Both were going to have to suffer one way or another every time they created something, or as we therapists say, "negotiated a new developmental stage." Like Eve, we all have to suffer the pain of giving birth to our autonomous selves. It's the payment for the "crime" of learning that we are not "one" with our mother, our father and later our mate and later still, our child, that we are separate and possessed with desires and needs often at odds with those of our nearest and dearest.

And so Adam and Eve—driven out of the womb of Eden and growing up and mating, creating, and dealing with the pain of existence and the knowledge of death—had a very hard time. Their little nuclear family didn't manage very well. Probably there was so much blame for losing Eden thrown back and forth, and work and pain having Cain and Abel and growing enough food for their greedy little mouths that we might say the family was downright dysfunctional. We know they never did learn how to reconcile Eros and Thanatos—that is love and hate, life and death—because things got so bad Cain killed Abel. The story doesn't tell us how Abel got to be the family victim and Cain the family murderer, but we can imagine the enmeshment, fights, and carrying on that went on in a household where the parents didn't know how to meet their own needs, much less each other's or their kids'. It's amazing that the family survived and eventually flourished enough so that the scribes of old Judea could write those long chapters of begats.

Back to the Present

Most of us manage, if by hook or by crook, to grow up being able to identify our feelings, process them, and take the appropriate action for our own self-interest. We are able to live happy, meaningful lives for ourselves with loving consideration of the needs of those we love, provided, of course, that we don't have a mass of inchoate rage and fear stemming from feeling like someone else's paltry rib, be it our mother's, our father's, or in turn, our mate's or children's.

That's why we like the other Genesis story of creation better. "Male and female created He them." There's no mention of poor Eve just being one of Adam's ribs and not her own separate self.

But the rib story does describe what it feels like to be born for someone else and not for ourselves.

If we believe on an unconscious level that we exist to fulfill the needs, ambitions, and desires of another, and that any needs, ambitions, or desires we might have that are different from what the other wants are bad, we will probably develop some sort of addiction. If, like Eve, we think we are created from another's rib, solely for another's fulfillment, we cannot tolerate our own desires. We can't even allow ourselves to realize they exist. So, like Eve, we reach fast for the apple.

More on How Our Culture Hurts Too

Today, in the industrialized nations for the most part, the pain of childbirth has been ameliorated. The problem of reaching for the apple has not. How we look, how we measure up to current standards of beauty is Eve's real curse. In some ages she was supposed to be fat, sleek, and well-fed. The unfortunate skinny girls were in misery. Today, the greatest gift a woman can have is a rapid metabolism and physical energy that makes her a "naturally thin" person. The girls with a tendency to be overweight are anxiously and constantly trying to be thinner. Even thin girls are trying to be thinner. The really fat girls are socially stigmatized and fairly miserable unless they have the ego strength and thick skin to be different from the beauty norm around them. The normal looking girls who are throwing up in secret to ward off the fat from binges they can't control are destroying their esophagi and self-esteem and endangering their health. Those thin girls dieting themselves into anorexia to avoid those hateful, painful, and forbidden feelings and terrors of the responsibility of adulthood are dying.

My Poor Mom and Me and My "Weight"

You know we like to teach by telling stories. Let me tell you a personal story. I deeply loved my mother. Despite what I am going to relate here, I still believe she was "one of the most wonderful women who ever lived" as we often say of mothers we honor. She was brave and strong. She stood up to Nazis in Germany and stopped a race riot in Michigan. She was the second woman reporter on the New York *American*. She was fun. She was witty. She experienced tragedies in her life, but she didn't let them get her down. She lost the fortune she had made on her own—an amazing feat for a woman—in the Depression. She rolled up her sleeves and went to work. Yes, she was something, my Mama. And she loved me with all her soul and all her heart. She did everything for me. She slaved to put me through the best schools but never made me feel guilty. "It's what I do for my child," she said. And that was the problem. I wasn't just her child. I was an extension of her. When she sent me to Vassar, she sent herself. It was as if I were her very flesh, her very hand. We were incredibly close. I was her confidant. She even let me listen at the head of the stairs to the grown-up talk and later explained to me anything I didn't understand. Her mother had been distant, hard, and mysterious, so my mama wasn't going to keep secrets from me. Her mother was cold. Mine would be warm; she would love me, and I would love her so much it would make up for every bad thing that ever happened. We would be best friends, in cahoots, facing life together, realizing her, and, therefore, my, dreams.

She was tall and gorgeous, with racehorse legs, great taste, a fine mind, and absolute surety that she knew what was right from politics to table settings. So I would be gorgeous, too, but not too tall as she felt her height had held her back as an actress. I, therefore, grew to what she thought was the perfect height, five foot four, and I was an actress. Naturally I was born with the right politics and a priori knowledge of the right forks simply because I was her daughter. In fact, she always used to say, "Never argue with people you have to teach." She never had to argue with me because she didn't have to teach me since I, she knew, thought and felt exactly as she did.

As long as we both thought her thoughts and felt her feelings, we were in bliss. I could even have all the thoughts and feelings she would have had if she had been my age, in my particular situation. My mommy and me. She often had to leave me to work. She would say to the baby sitter when she left, "treat my child with love, I don't care what else you do." I knew my world was to be wonderful and perfect because my mommy said so. She was my all-powerful, beautiful, gardenia-smelling world in her physical presence and in my spirit even when she wasn't actually with me.

There was only one problem. Sometimes when no one was looking I would eat spoons of sugar from the bowl. She would see the evidence sprinkled on the living room carpet. We would both wonder why I had done such a thing. After all, she told me I didn't like sugar. All I knew was that I had to have that sugar.

Clinically, I now know that whenever I had the tension of a desire, a thought, a longing different from hers or not approved of by her, I grabbed food. That was one of the contributors to my weight problem. That's not the point of this story except to stress that addiction to food was the only means I had to deal with what was different in me from "the most wonderful woman in the world."

My mother died. I grew up. If I were my patient, I would say that by keeping my weight problem, I've kept her alive all these years. But I probably wouldn't say that to a patient because it never does any good to tell people what's wrong with them. Suffice it to say that after decades of yo-yo dieting, I've made my accommodation to a symptom I can't or won't give up. Today, I eat what I want. Although I really like food, I don't eat as much as some gloriously thin people I know. Nevertheless, since I gave up dieting, I am enormous. So what? My blood pressure is 120 over

80, and my cholesterol and triglyceride numbers are good. Except for being "morbidly obese," I am quite healthy, and my bone density is fabulous. When I get tired of buying clothes at the fat stores, think it might be fun to run a mile, decide I would like to be thin again, and am willing to make the trade-offs that effort requires, I will probably lose weight. For me that will be an excruciatingly difficult task. I may have to tackle it in order to avoid future health problems. The point of telling my story is to set out an example of the emotional etiology that contributes to obesity. I learned to grab a substance whenever I had feelings that were separate and therefore unacceptable to my beloved Mother. If she had been stupid, cruel, mean, unattractive, cowardly, selfish, mendacious, I would have had an easy time of separating[2] my feelings and my life from hers. If she had known more about how children need to separate from their parents, she would have helped me. If she had lived, that woman who would have fought wild tigers to keep me from harm, I am sure, with help, would have let me go to be me, not her. She would have had the courage to learn that love that goes beyond the boundaries of the beloved's selfhood causes emotional illness.

But let me repeat here, there are other factors in eating disorders besides the parent–child relationship. I no longer have a hard time recognizing feelings that I feel are in some way unacceptable and no longer feel the need to grab for something to squelch them before I know what they are. I still, however, have the fat cells that want to fill up, the metabolism that would keep me alive without food in the Arctic for six months while everyone else was dead, and a real liking for cooking and food. I also get just plain hungry. I do not like being hungry. I am not willing anymore to feel deprived so I can fit into the American ideal. So, I'm a fat older woman rather than a wizened one. If anybody has

---

2. The word "separate" as used in this book concerns the transition when a child matures to become a young adult of the family. These are psychological stages. What is known as "separation/individuation" should happen during adolescence. Sometimes it doesn't happen until a person is in her or his 30s or 40s. Sometimes it never happens at all.

a problem with how I look, it's their problem and not mine. They can deal with it. At this juncture, I am for the most part content with being a very beautiful, very fat, very active sixty-two-year-old woman who gets to eat very good dinners. Of course, I would like to be lithe, lovely, and forty-two. Well, we can't have everything. So I think of my eating disorder as a handicap that I do not allow to impinge on my life. I do not isolate myself. I work. I see friends. I write. I see patients. I study psychoanalysis. I love. I nurture my family in that I am always available to them and in that I provide them with family rituals. I am in awe of my glorious grandchildren; I adore them. But I always remember they are my daughter's babies and not mine. When I get an attack of self-pity, I think about Franklin Delano Roosevelt guiding this country through World War II from a wheelchair. Then I put on my face, get rigged out in my best clothes, and get going, get doing. (I adore makeup and clothes and buy them at the best fat shops in town.)

However, being human, I sometimes feel guilty that I do not fit into the norm. I sometimes have a hard time remembering that there are still physiological, chemical, political, and societal factors, as well as issues of enmeshment and control that contribute to my eating disorder. I am sorry that very large, very powerful, very female women make other people uncomfortable. Now that feminism has made strides and women are gaining more power, our society is ambivalent. We've come a long way, baby, but people prefer us not to look like it. Hide the power. Hide the femaleness. Look like little boys, small, muscular, not pregnant, and very young. Wear great big clodhopper shoes. Sometimes when I slip into my little patent leather sandals and spray on perfume that is not a scent for both sexes, I feel wrong, uncomfortable, even alien. I sometimes can feel disapproval wafting toward me. I suppose if and when looking like me becomes more uncomfortable than spending two hours at a gym every day, eating rabbit food, and making "health" my life's work, I will probably curl up and diet.

All I know is that if an obese person like myself exercises, limits her food intake, goes to psychotherapist, an over-eaters group, a psychiatrist, and a reliable internist who specializes in eating disorders, I may be able to lose weight. Note the word "may." Progress is being made every day. I have no doubt that eventually we will understand all the factors that make some people fat and others thin. Until then, as I said, fat people need the courage of Joan of Arc to make the society they live in treasure and respect them and realize they have other qualities besides FAT. And the biggest hurdle I will have to overcome is the painfully and deeply rooted desire not to be thin.

A girl asked Dr. Carol Broad once if her bulimia could be "cured." Dr. Broad asked her if she wanted to be cured. The girl looked startled and paused before she said, "That is some question. I honestly don't know. I do my bulimic thing and the tension is gone."

Nothing can help one reach the norm of weight and dealing with food unless the true, real desire is there. Often unconscious factors sabotage this desire.

Like the young woman in Dr. Broad's office, I still don't know if I want to be cured. That's just where I am today.

But one thing is for sure: *I did not want to pass my weight problem on to my children.* With the help of a therapist, I worked very hard at it. That work mostly consisted of regarding them always as separate beings from me. If I did nothing else for them, I tried to teach them that they were not me and I was not them. They, not I, owned their souls, minds, and bodies. When one of them once complained to me that she was fat, (a big ten pounds overweight) I said "Darling, I'm not good at that subject so you'll have to get help from someone else." She did.

What I did was to try to keep food from being as big an issue for them as it was for me. I always had loads of good food in the house and never denied them junk food so that it would not become the "forbidden joy." I did not use food as a reward or punishment. Of course, since I liked food so much, they do, too. But at least for them, it is a pleasure and not an addiction. This was the best I could do. They have their own lives, their own problems, their own solutions. They will just have to "deal" as they say. And so will I. So far, so good. My daughters seem to be free of eating problems and don't worry about thinness any more than most women their age. They, of course, worry a lot. After all, they are American women living in the media and fashion center of the world and are barraged by the message BE THIN from every magazine, TV show, movie, store, job, activity, man, woman, and child over the age of three they encounter. They, like everyone in America know it is their aesthetic duty to do all in their power to look like somebody's fourteen-year-old brother. They know, as does every woman in America from the age of four to ninety that being fat is as un-American as apple pie used to be American. Fortunately, they also seem to have inherited their father's metabolism. They also did not have as babies the same feelings of hunger that I had. Truly, they got a better serving of lean genes than I did. What other factors operated in their not being eating-disordered, I don't know.

With parts of my story, I am merely trying to show where most food addictions start, how the substance of food or any addictive substance for that matter becomes a substitute for autonomy and feelings the Eves of addiction dare not have. I have shown that eating disorders are also a societal problem emanating from our culture every bit as much as from our families. In order to help our children, we have to know and change our part in their illness, but we also have to do all in our power to combat the beauty ideal of slimness that is impossible for so many of our daughters to meet.

What My Mom Didn't Know

As I said previously, if my beloved mother had known that she was sowing the seeds of neurosis in me, she would have done her level best to change her behavior towards me.

She would have taught me that I was not her, that I was me.

She would have allowed me to have separate feelings and opinions from hers without being hurt to the quick.

She would have let me solve my problems, not our problems.

She would have told me school was my job not hers (i.e., she would not have stood over me correcting my homework every night).

She would not have trained me to be an actress to redeem her lost career.

She would have let me part my hair on the side rather than the middle because it was my hair, not hers, and I should have had a chance to wear it as I liked.

She would have set up some boundaries between us as adult and child.

She would have learned not to think of me as an extension of her; I would not have been as much a part of her as her own hand.

She would have learned to love me without loving me as herself.

At five foot seven, she would not have had to weigh what she wanted me to weigh at five foot four.

She did not have to eat what she wanted me to eat. She could have indulged in the peach ice-cream sundaes with caramel sauce that she loved.

She would not have met me at the train from school saying, "Oh, my God, you're 133-you've-gained-ten-pounds-you-mustn't-see-anybody-till-we've-got-them-off-we-just-won't-let-anybody-know-you're-home-till-they're-off."

WE always dieted ME. Once, when my mother came to visit me in New York, I had gained twenty pounds. I could only manage to gain weight when I was away from her. I was in rebellion. I met her plane wearing my husband's old army fatigues and clogs. I had my long blonde hair loose with little Brunhilde braids streaming down my face. I looked like some Valkyrie ready to foment revolution. I was wearing my husband's clothes partly because I had been taught never to buy new clothes when I was overweight, and I had fatted out of my wardrobe. As we got out of the taxi from the airport, she stumbled, grabbed the side of the building, and started to pant. A lean, pathetic figure in her navy-blue suit, white gloves, pearls, and pin, she seemed to me in my hippie soldier garb to be having a heart attack.

"Mummy," I cried, "let me help! I'll get an ambulance!"

"It's nothing, darling. It's just I can't bear the way you look. We'll be all right when we change your clothes and we get you dieted."

She would not have had to rewrite my first book and throw away the original. She could have written a book of her own. She would have felt guilty when she read my diaries and my mail because she would have know they weren't hers.

I believe she wouldn't have done these things had she known. I believe she would have worked through her own narcissism, no matter how painful a process it was, if she had known she had it. She truly loved me and wanted to do the best for me. I believe that the parents who read this book will work through their narcissism, too, because they truly love their children, want to do the best for them, and are willing to work hard to do it.

6

Money, Yes or No? If Yes, How Much?

Money talks. If you listen, it will tell you an astonishing amount about you and your family because, along with sex, money is the place where we all "act out."

"Acting out," of course, is the expression of emotion in an action rather than in words. Instead of saying that we are angry, disappointed, or sad we *do* something. Now, we all know that understanding each other when we speak clearly to one another in words is difficult enough, but when feelings are expressed in body language or in action, the communication is really very easily misunderstood.

Acting out may express emotions of which we are conscious — we know we're miserable and we're reacting because we are — or unconscious, feelings with which we are not in touch and of which we are totally unaware. But whether the emotions being expressed are conscious or unconscious, acting them out is apt to cause confusion or sadness or pain or anger or some or all of the above. A tremendous amount of mischief is especially caught up in acting out with money, and it will be the purpose of this chapter to explore some of the more common difficulties and their remedies.

In the best of all possible worlds there would be no hidden agenda in the way we manage money—no acting out. Instead, we would be open, fair, generous when we were able to do so, good shepherds of our resources when we were not.

We would recognize our impulses to act out and put feelings into words in an appropriate manner, thereby gaining control over those feelings. In other words, we would be aware of our unconscious impulses to use money to hurt, to control, to bribe. What a grand world that would be! What pain we would be spared! What rages would never happen!

Unfortunately, we are all imperfect human beings with powerful conscious and unconscious emotional instruments. Our conscious feelings push us openly toward acting out, but we have some awareness of what we're doing. Our unconscious feelings, on the other hand, are much more mischievous because they drive us relentlessly while we remain unaware of their existence.

Sometimes, when our children have driven us up the wall and we're really angry, *consciously* angry, instead of saying so, we withhold money. We try to hurt back ("Loan? I'm not even going to talk about a loan!") or to punish, ("Teach her to earn her own money!"). On other occasions, when our children cause us to be consciously frightened, instead of saying so, we give money ("Here. Take a taxi instead of the bus.") and in so doing, attempt to placate or possibly to bribe.

In either case, we're using money to express conscious feelings—anger or fear in these instances—and, in some way, to control. But emotions are far better expressed in words—in an appropriate manner and setting where we can achieve the best results for all concerned. And that's when we're dealing with conscious feelings.

What about unconscious forces in the handling of money? Very often, the fact that there is an unconscious price tag on a present of money is absolutely unknown to us.

Let's look at a case.

One of our patients, Stephen, is a father who generously gives gifts of money to his children and, when he does so, feels he is being a loving father. He is completely unaware of any ulterior motives; all he wants is to "help out the kids." His motto is "an open wallet and a closed mouth." Because Stephen's real motives for his generosity are hidden in his unconscious mind, he remains oblivious to them. He doesn't recognize that in his generosity he is "acting out" an unconscious wish to be loved by his children. Rather than generosity, his presents of money represent efforts to buy, seduce, control, and get for himself.

There's nothing terribly wrong in wanting to be loved, but because Stephen's feelings are being acted out instead of being put into words, his children are confused. Stephen has told them there are no strings attached to his gifts of money, but the kids sense there is something more. Their problem is that they don't know exactly what; they don't realize there's a very powerful expectation attached to their father's presents: love in some form, preferably as gratitude. And if that gratitude is not forthcoming, or is provided in less than the desired amounts, as unhappily is often the case, Stephen is injured or even inflamed—and there is a spasm of trouble in the family. Hurt feelings, family members not talking to one another, a deep sense of being misunderstood, unappreciated, all of which are very painful.

Some unconscious wishes are not so benign as a simple desire to be loved. Let's go to the other end of the spectrum.

In chapter 4, we talked about how an enabler, in giving money to an addict, is really helping the addict stay addicted. Enablers are almost always distraught, confused, and convinced in their conscious minds that they are being helpful when they give money to an addict. What are they achieving when they do so? They're helping keep the addict addicted. And the consequences of addiction are very harmful and, ultimately, may lead to death.

A psychoanalyst will usually assume that whatever outcome results from an action represents an unconscious wish. In a situation involving an enabler, it will be theorized that the enabler is so angry at the addict that the unconscious wish is to harm or kill.

So acting out can range from minor to major acts. Some acting out—like giving money in hopes of getting affection in return— may only upset family relationships. Other forms of acting out—giving money to an addict—can be extremely hurtful, even deadly.

None of these outcomes is desirable, and there is nothing that says they must always exist. We are not made of concrete. We are all capable of change. Let us operate on the theory that acting out an unconscious emotion (usually involving a wish) in the handling of money can many times be avoided.

The questions that get most of us parents are usually: (1) *if* to give money; (2) *when* to give money; (3) *how much* money to give; and (4) *what it is reasonable to expect in return*. But we cannot even go near those questions until we are satisfied that we have explored our own conscious and unconscious investments in money and what its uses mean to us; i.e. are we acting out and if so, how?"

In examining how money is handled within a family, there is only one place where we as parents can begin and that is our own childhoods. How did our moms and dads handle money when we were little? It's very easy to dismiss that question with a joke— "What money?" Or an easy generalization—"It was never an issue" Or—"We never thought about it," "there wasn't any other subject for discussion, we were so poor." When we hear ourselves making one of those responses we can recognize how painful or frightening or infuriating it is to open up those old histories. We'd rather dismiss the subject with a quip.

In the same way that an addict is invited to make a "fearless and searching moral inventory" of his or her addiction, when there are money problems in a family, parents must make a "fearless and searching *financial* inventory" of their own histories.

The question, of course, is what were we taught when we were little. If money was used as a form of acting out in our childhoods, what feelings were being expressed? Was money used to punish? To reward? As bait? To imprison? What did we learn at our parents' knees?

We live in reaction to our childhoods. Most of us think that we are rational human beings making rational decisions about money; but when we look back at the way our parents handled money, we are often shocked to find, that while we disagreed with their methods, we are doing the same thing today. Or we're doing exactly the opposite, which is really the same thing: we're still dancing to their piper.

If you are a mother or father who can safely enjoy a glass of wine, would you consider sitting down and trying to remember? (Coffee will do just as well. The idea is to have a little nurturing for yourself while you go back into an ancient history that can be disturbing.) If you're a single parent, borrow a friend who will listen to you *without being critical*. Take some time to allow the wine (or coffee) to help your memory—which it will do for some people—and talk. Reminisce about the financial ghosts in your past. Were your parents generous? Were they stingy? Why? Why not? Take your time. Don't try to work it out in five or ten minutes but really ruminate. You'll be surprised at the memories, feelings, and ideas that can come to the surface if you're patient. A sudden recall of an allowance being canceled because the lawn wasn't mowed properly. Or the angry recollection of the child for whom clothing money couldn't be found. Or the slow filtering back of the feelings aroused by being given half as much spending money as the other kids in your class—when money in the household was not a problem; a sense that you weren't considered worth being provided with money. Take some time. You may explore this material over a period of weeks as feelings and memories come trickling back. It's interesting work, if not always comfortable.

When you've explored your own childhood and the way money was managed back then you'll have some idea of how you're expected to behave in the here-and-now. The unconscious pressure to "do to them what was done to us" is much greater than most of us realize. And it happens in every family.

The starting point, then, is to know more about ourselves, which isn't always easy. In fact, parents sometimes need help in coming to terms with their own financial ghosts.

Let's look at another case in point.

Martin, now fifty, happily married for twenty-five years, and the father of three, is the son of a charming, fast-talking, up-by-his-bootstraps salesman who left home when he was seventeen. In the middle of the Depression, Martin's father began selling cleaning supplies door to door and rose to have his own carpet cleaning business, which became large and prosperous. Martin was always in awe of his self-made father—who had begun with nothing and built a great success without help from anyone—and had difficulty standing up to him.

When Martin was a teenager, he dreamed of joining the merchant marine, of sailing across boundaryless expanses of ocean, of weather, sky, and romance. His father, then graying and putting on weight, wanted him to take over the family business and gave him an ultimatum: if Martin went off to sea he would never see a penny of the family money. The business was his *if* he was willing to work for it. If he wasn't willing, then Martin's father proposed to sell the business and live high off the proceeds, timing things so that the exhaustion of his funds and his own death would occur together. Martin would get nothing.

What was really going on? What was the feeling that was being acted out by Martin's father in his ultimatum to his son? The public statement that Martin must work for his share in the business was not the real issue. Beware of those simplistic assertions. People speaking from the moral high ground are seldom dealing in truth. What was not being put into words, quite simply, was that Martin's father, as the result of his own childhood, was fearful of abandonment. He was going to make damn sure his son didn't walk out on him the way he had walked out on his own father. That, of course, was an unconscious process, never in consciousness, and in consequence never put into words.

At the time, Martin considered his alternatives and then, filled with shame at his own weakness, gave up his dreams of a life at sea and went into the family business. Not only was he deprived of the career he wanted, but for twenty-seven years he had to work for his father (who lived to be very old and sat in his office until three days before he died), a lifetime of being provided with small amounts of praise and large amounts of fault-finding. No matter how well Martin did, his father found something lacking. Martin loved his father but hated working for him. It was torture, it was misery, and it colored most of his adult life. The small sailboat he kept on a nearby lake did not compensate for the life at sea he had never had.

It is thirty years later, and now it is Martin who is gray and twenty-five pounds overweight and aware that more of his life is behind him than is ahead of him. And, curiously, he has an adored son, Arnold, as well as two daughters, and the same story is being reenacted. The family business—thanks to Martin's expansion into franchising—is now an industrial giant. But Martin—like his father before him—fears abandonment and is insisting that his son come into the business with him. His reasoning is the same as his father's. *He* had to work for *his* share of the business and, if Arnold is to have a share, *he* must do likewise. The unconscious feeling, of course, is that Martin never had what he wanted during his working life; at least, he can have his children around him in his final years, certainly an understandable desire. Despite its being all so obvious, Martin is unaware that he is doing to his own son exactly what was done to him so many years before.

Martin loves Arnold and wants to do what is right by him. He's told Arnold he can do anything he chooses and if his choice happens to include the family empire that's fine with Martin. He won't, however, help Arnold in any substantive manner to find his own way *outside* the family business. If Arnold comes into the family business the world is his oyster; if he goes elsewhere, he's pretty much on his own. Martin holds up his own father as an example of "getting ahead on your own," and Arnold burns with anger.

Martin has been giving Arnold what we call a split message. In words he tells his son that he is free to choose any career for himself he likes; but in the withholding of money, Martin's unconscious message is that he is furious at the idea of Arnold leaving him. These split messages are very confusing and cause endless amounts of trouble.

Arnold has a history of depression and has been in and out of therapy. He wants to be in a filmmaker and now owes substantial payments on school loans he took when he decided to get an M.F.A. in film. (Martin refused to help him with what he viewed as a "frivolous" graduate degree.) Arnold has worked around the periphery of the movie business and lived poor, as movie people usually do. Yet he has never relinquished his claim to his share in the family business. If the film business doesn't work out for him, he says, the family business might be just right. He just wants to give it his "best shot." His father's upper lip often curls at the mention of the movie industry.

Martin's ever-so-slightly contemptuous attitude toward show business continually drives Arnold away from the family business and toward the film world. It also usually leaves Arnold depressed. Every couple of months, Martin sends Arnold a check—not a very big one but one on which his son has come to rely and which invariably bails him out. Each check is a reminder that if Arnold ever decides to come home he will have all the money he needs. It is also a reminder that he has failed to become self-sufficient, to "stand on his own two feet."

To add to the family misery, Arnold's two sisters work for their father—as do both their husbands—and they will all be perfectly happy if Arnold waives his share of the business and stays away in the world of film.

The difficulty in this family is that what is *not* being said is poisoning the personal relationships. Martin is feeling abandoned by his son and finds fault with him exactly as his own father found fault with him. It is an unconscious process, another repetition, of which he is unaware.

Arnold is feeling abandoned by his father, and his depressions are more frequent and more troublesome. He is slowly coming to despise his father, without ever being quite sure why. After all, there are those checks. The two men quarrel, often about trivial matters, and neither is quite sure why.

Arnold's sisters side with their father and complain about their brother getting checks for which he doesn't work. Whenever Arnold comes home for a visit, they lord their material possessions over the starving filmmaker, and he is now starting to despise them, as well.

Arnold's mother tries to make peace—and cries.

Despite all the financial affluence, theirs is a fragmented and unhappy family. Arnold's father, Martin, is angry and frustrated; Arnold's mother is miserable. Arnold's sisters resent him, and he resents them. Holidays—an unspoken requirement if Arnold is to continue to receive the checks—are tense and argumentative. The whole family is tortured. And yet they are all nice people.

They could have gone on this way—everything important under the surface, nothing put into words, with money the principal irritant—except that after a particularly painful confrontation with his father, Arnold went upstairs to his bedroom and took an overdose of tranquilizers. Arnold's mother

recognized her son's suicide attempt as a cry for help and proposed that the family go for therapy.

The immediate reaction to her suggestion was that the only
problem in the family was Arnold. *He* was the one who should get
therapy. Martin certainly agreed; he didn't have the time and
didn't see the need. His son should go. Arnold's sisters contended
the problem was his and his alone and had nothing to do with
them. Arnold himself thought he was the only one with a problem.

But when Arnold came into therapy, we suggested that the
problem was a family problem and, in time, the whole family—
including Arnold's two brothers-in-law—were assembled in a
family therapy session.

It was a bloodletting. Fearing that therapy would lead to Arnold's
leaving home permanently, Martin lost his temper and screamed
at his son for being a dreamer and a malingerer. Arnold lashed
back, snarling that his father was trying to control his whole life.
Martin was deeply hurt. Arnold's sisters then defended their father,
and Arnold snarled at them in turn. Now they shrieked at him. His
brothers-in-law denounced him with cold contempt. Arnold lost
his temper and called them "a pair of lousy fortune hunters."
Arnold's mother cried.

As the session went on, some truths began to be put into words,
and people usually recognize the truth when they hear it from
their own mouths.

By the end of the session, Martin had begun to realize that he
was playing a role in his son's illness; Arnold's sisters had begun
to face the fact that sibling rivalry and their own common greed
was no small part of the problem; and Arnold himself had begun
to see that his indecisiveness about being in the family business or
out of the family business was a big contributing factor.

It was strange for the members of the family to realize, when
they left that first session, that despite all of the terrible feelings
that had been felt and the words that had been spoken, they felt
better, relieved, actually, and more comfortable with each other.

In the following sessions, the real truths had to be spoken and faced. Martin had to come to acknowledge his dependency on Arnold and how much he wanted him in the family business. Arnold's mother had to admit that she had a special interest in Arnold's career in films because it was a career she had wanted for herself when she was young. Arnold's sisters had to confess their feelings that their mother preferred her only son to them, as did their father. They had to concede that they liked Arnold away from the business because then they felt they got their fair share of their parents' attention. Arnold's brothers-in-law had to admit the humiliation they felt—and the anger—when Martin, like his son, treated them with lightly veiled contempt. Talking and talking and talking—with some analytic counseling—helped the family begin to deal with feelings in words rather than acting out.

After many sessions—when all the feelings had been faced—it was possible to work out a here-and-now compromise. Martin had come to realize that he was doing the same hateful thing to his son that had been done to him, and he knew that wasn't right.

When Arnold gave his father the feeling that he loved him and wanted to be part of his life even if he wasn't living at home, Martin was able to let him go. Martin gave up using the family money as bait for a trap. The profits of the company were redivided so that Arnold and his sisters would each receive the same share every year.

That division gave Arnold enough money to pursue his life as a filmmaker. His sisters and their husbands would continue to draw salaries for their work, which gave them the recognition and affluence so important to them. With money no longer being used as a leash to control him, Arnold felt closer to his father. They agreed to talk a couple of times a week on the phone and see each other regularly. Martin's fear that he would be abandoned by his son was put into words and then put to rest.

When the true nature of the conflict is resolved, money is seldom the real problem, but it is certainly a problem presented to parents in many forms. Let's look at another case.

We met Ken and Alicia through their eighteen-year-old daughter, Melissa. Her pretty face streaked by twin smears of mascara streaming down her cheeks, Melissa came rushing into our office one afternoon and was instantly in hysterics. She announced that she had no money and that we had to help her; otherwise, she would look for the nearest bridge. (One of our other patients had sent her to us.)

We suggested that before we attempted to deal with the money issue—which we suspected was not an issue at all—she sit down, take a few deep breaths, and then tell us what was going on in her life.

Melissa did so, but the anger that drove her tears was unabated. "I'm the good one," she announced.

The story she told was troublesome in many ways.

While Melissa was a junior in high school, her older sister, Kimberly, then in her freshman year at a local college, came home announcing she was pregnant. The father of her child was a foreign exchange student who quickly went home and dropped out of sight. When Kimberly brought her problem to Ken and Alicia, all agreed that abortion was not a solution acceptable to them. It was difficult emotionally and financially, but the family elected to concentrate on the realities of the situation to the exclusion of everything else, which means that they dealt in the practical issues at hand and did not deal in the many feelings that were aroused by Kimberly's pregnancy.

Ken and Alicia both work for the city in middle management jobs that have not permitted them to build up substantial savings. For many years, they painfully set aside money for Kimberly's and Melissa's college—but there was nothing extra. Nevertheless, faced with Kimberly's pregnancy, they determined to rally around. They brought Kimberly home from college and saw her through her confinement. When the baby was born—and all agreed it was a wonderful baby, indeed—Melissa moved out of the bedroom she had shared with Kimberly all her life and onto the living room couch. Kimberly and the baby had the bedroom.

The addition of a baby in that small apartment created constant tension. The apartment was overcrowded and one result was constant quarreling. Ken and Alicia, who prided themselves on being reasonable people, felt the situation to be untenable, so they rented a small apartment nearby for Kimberly and the baby. At least that got Melissa off the living room couch.

They had to face the painful prospect that Kimberly would have to raise their grandchild without the help of a husband. To help Kimberly acquire the skills that would enable her to support herself and her child, they arranged for child care and sent her back to college. The additional money for child care came, of course, from the funds they had put away for Melissa's education. But what else could they do?

As Melissa's high school graduation approached, Ken and Alicia had to face their own financial realities. They would no longer be able to pay for college for both girls. Melissa would have to get a full-time job and go to college at night, if she was to go at all. It was not a decision that made Ken and Alicia happy. They knew it was unfair to Melissa, but the money they were giving to Kimberly was for *both* her and their grandchild. Surely they should do the best they could for them?

Melissa was overwhelmed with a profound sense of injustice — and it was one such hysterical scene that led her to us. After meeting with us twice, she asked if she could bring her parents with her for the next session. We suggested that, if they were willing, her parents might phone us and discuss the possibility of family therapy. The next day Ken phoned and we arranged for him and Alicia to come in for a marital session to be followed by family therapy that would include both Melissa *and* Kimberly.

That session with Ken and Alicia proved to be very difficult. Both were intensely troubled by the situation and intensely defensive. They were desperately sad about Kimberly's situation and guilty about what they saw as their unfair treatment of Melissa. But what else could they do? There wasn't money to help Kimberly with an apartment and with child care—neither of which was cheap—and send both girls to college. If they could send only one girl, wasn't the right thing to do to help Kimberly get "business training" so she could support her baby? How would it make sense to punish Kimberly and, in effect, punish their grandchild as well, by taking her out of school and allowing Melissa to go instead? Would refusing to send either of them to college be any more fair?

Ken and Alicia both cried with frustration. Ken left feeling like a failure because he didn't have more money. Alicia wept for her children and her grandchild.

Those were the feelings they brought into the room at the first session and those were the feelings that filled the room when they left. Yet they elected to come back for another marital session before bringing in their daughters. But the marital session— which became sessions—seemed fruitless. Five sessions came and went with only the same litany of guilt and confusion, but somewhat to our surprise, Ken and Alicia, despite the lack of progress we seemed to be making, kept wanting to come back.

We theorized between ourselves that there was something they wanted to tell us and told each other we must be patient. Sure enough, in our sixth session Ken's truth emerged in the form of a joke.

One of us had asked him a question that had been asked many times in many different forms during our work together: in view of the strain it put on their family finances, what had led them to the decision to put Kimberly into her own apartment and send her back to college as well?

"Well, it was either college or kill her," blurted out Ken with a great smile and a laugh.

Psychoanalysts are trained to understand that kind of impulsive joke as a statement of unconscious truth. For the first time Ken had acknowledged the murderous rage ("or kill her") he felt toward Kimberly for her sexual misbehavior and for getting pregnant. They were certainly understandable feelings, and we were relieved that he had finally touched upon them.

We simply asked him to explore that statement. Our noncritical acceptance of his feelings then led to an emotional outpouring from Ken in which Alicia joined. Both parents were in a fury at the behavior of their older daughter, in whom they had invested so many hopes and dreams. What was startling was that they had never before acknowledged those feelings, even to each other. They had admitted sadness and dismay but never outrage and fury. Instead they had acted out their angry feelings —but not directly. When emotions are acted out, they often emerge in almost unrecognizable forms. In this instance, the unconscious rage at Kimberly was accompanied with a fear of loss. If Ken's impulse to kill Kimberly became reality, he would lose her, and losing her would be a loss he could not endure. The fear of loss, separation, or abandonment underlies many of our unconsciously driven actions. So the unconscious did one of its tricks. It converted the impulse to kill into the impulse to preserve. Ken found himself obsessed with the feeling that they must stand by Kimberly and help her in every way. Even when he was out looking for an apartment for her, he knew he was being unfair to Melissa, but the unconscious is a powerful master, and he was driven to care for Kimberly.

In this session, Ken faced his own rage and murderous impulses toward Kimberly, putting them into words with us. Once they were in words, they were largely gone, and he could look at the situation with more objectivity. Where he had been driven by unconscious impulses before, now his rational mind was far more in charge. The psychoanalytic wisdom says that "when the unconscious is made conscious, change starts." Now it was time for the girls to be brought in for another family session. It began as a very unhappy experience. The situation was not what anyone had wanted, and yet some positives did emerge from it: there was a beautiful baby, and the family was intact.

But there remained problems that had not been solved. After much talking, in which all their feelings were taken into consideration, the family living arrangements were readjusted. Kimberly agreed to give up her apartment and move back home with her baby and go to college at night. When she was away at school, her mother and/or her father would babysit. Melissa agreed to resume sleeping on the living room couch until it was time for her to go off to college, and then she, indeed, would go to a sleep-away college as had been the original family expectation. She also agreed to get loans and scholarships to ease the burden on her family. That felt fair to her, and she was only too glad to help her sister when she could. Ken and Alicia felt they had arrived at a situation with which they could live. It wasn't perfect. It wasn't what they had hoped for, but it was reasonable, and they knew they were doing the best they could for both their daughters.

Let us go back to the original questions with which we began this chapter: *if* to give money, *when* to give money, *how much* money to give, and *what it is reasonable to expect* in return. Since every family is unique, there are no universal answers to these questions, and yet there is a universal answer.

If your goal for your children is that they become independent, self-supporting, and autonomous, then money should be invested toward those goals. Money should be shared with children in an appropriate manner, providing, when we are fortunate enough to be able to do so, enough financial assistance to help them become independent of us and self-supporting.

The danger, always, is an unconscious desire to keep our children with us, in service, dependent on us. It is difficult for the unconscious to accept the idea that children can grow up and become independent and still remain close to us.

Our goal, of course, is to help our children go through a maturational process in which they will change from being the children of the family to become the young adults of the family.

What is called in psychological language a process of separation/indivuation does not mean parents are to lose their children. Rather, their children are to progress from being dependent on us to being independent of us while remaining within the family.

If we are aware of our own unconscious impulses to keep our children tied to us, and *if* we are willing to allow them to mature into independent adults, *then* we can avoid using money in a way that is crippling.

The tragedy of parents who are so needy that they must continually give gifts of money to their children in order to destroy their children's chances for independence is far too frequent. Such acting out of the fear of abandonment is far better dealt with in a therapist's office than inflicted on young people who often cannot defend themselves.

Frequently, this situation is repeated in generation after generation. It does not have to be. The fear of abandonment can be faced and overcome, and our children can be assisted rather than hindered in their steps toward autonomy. We can reap the reward of knowing that we have produced strong, loving, independent, grown-up children of whom we can be proud.

In giving or withholding money, the key question is always "what's in it for me?" Is a gift—or the refusal of a gift—serving a parent's purposes, or does it say "I love you. I respect you. This is to help you become the fine adult I know you can be. God speed."

7

If Your Kid's Love Seems to You All Wrong

If you have a kid who is willing to be guided by you in his or her selection of a lover or mate, something has gone terribly wrong. And if that sentence has to be explained, something has gone terribly wrong.

This chapter is for all the parents who have been watching their kids—often with affection and hope, other times with dismay and even disbelief—go through the courtship years, trying out various possible life companions. It is a difficult time for all of us. Sometimes, in the beginning, many of us make the mistake of getting attached to this young man or that young girl, perhaps far too attached, and suddenly find, to our intense disappointment, that the young man or young girl has suddenly and totally disappeared from our life.

Sometimes, all our worries turn to happiness when our kid settles on a really fine young person, and we are able to heave a sigh of relief. We foresee a lifetime of happiness and accomplishment for our kid, and all is well in our world. (Jackie Onassis really had it right when she said that if your kids weren't okay nothing else mattered very much.)

But other times, it does happen that our kid makes a choice which really alarms us, distresses us, or, in some cases, causes us intense pain. Those are situations that attack long-standing personal relationships and values and sometimes tear families apart—and it is to those unhappy family situations that this chapter is devoted.

Let's start with one of the simpler situations, one to which we may very well have an answer—the inappropriate companion to whom your kid is not yet married. Since the vows have not been taken, that means you have some time, and where there is time, there is usually hope.

Now what do we mean by "inappropriate"? Perhaps the simplest answer is to say that an inappropriate companion is anyone whom you feel is wrong for your kid—too old, too young, too educated, too uneducated, too moral, too immoral, too rich, too poor, too polite, too rude, of the wrong class, of the wrong faith, of the wrong race, or wrong in some way that troubles you deeply.

Do you have the right to intervene in any way? A very good question. Most of us try to treat our grown kids as adults—as a way of helping them *become* adults. Certainly, you have read again and again in this book our distaste for the dreaded unsolicited advice. Yet there are times when our hearts are in our mouths, when we see a lover or companion who fills us with dismay and whom we really would like to see gone from our lives. Well, there is a way of interfering without interfering. Especially if they aren't married. Not yet married does provide an opportunity. (These situations become much more difficult, as all our readers understand, when they are married and when there are children.) As you probably have noticed by now, we like to present our ideas and theories through stories because we think that's a good way to stimulate thought and perhaps be persuasive. But in this chapter presenting stories is unusually difficult. There are so many ways in which kids can be wrong for each other, so many ways in which parents can become deeply troubled, incensed, furious, that this is clearly a subject that resists generalization. However, we've elected to continue with our story telling because the principles of dealing with these situations—as with almost all of the situations we are presenting in this book—remain constant.

Consider the situation that faced Donald and Doris, two very well-intentioned, bright, highly educated parents. Education was the center of their world. Donald was a professor of mathematics at the local university, and Doris headed up the science department at the local high school. Both of them prided themselves on being rational, and both thought of themselves as being reasonable. Ha!

While they had six daughters the oldest, Eloise, (secretly, because they tried to be even-handed with all the girls) had always been special in their eyes. A quick mind, a great memory, recently graduated from college Phi Beta Kappa, and wondering what to do next, Eloise was under considerable pressure from her parents to make a decision, to choose a direction for her life, and, above all, to pick a graduate school. Any graduate school. To Donald and Doris, graduate school was the ticket to future success, to social status, to the "right" man. To them, graduate school was everything. You can imagine Donald's and Doris' delight, then, when Eloise, struggling to hold herself together under all the family pressures, went to a cookout and fell in love with Ben, a full-fledged member of the Hell's Angels.

Ben was big, bearded, boisterous, and didn't suffer fools. He had a reputation for drinking and fighting, although with Eloise he was indeed 'a lamb.' While it was true that he had barely managed to earn a high school general equivalency diploma (GED), and he had a work record that at best could be called "spotty," he also had self assurance and great personal charm. There was more. Not only was Ben a member of a notorious motorcycle gang, but he celebrated that membership—and a few antisocial attitudes—by numerous tattoos that ornamented prominent parts of his body. Most prominent was a slogan on the left side of his neck, just above the collar line (although, truth to tell, he rarely wore a shirt with a collar) instructing the world to KILL FOR JESUS!, a sentiment designed to be inflammatory and one that succeeded almost beyond measure with Donald.

Eloise couldn't have made a better choice. Ben was everything her father hated, and everything that made her mother weep. And in a curious way, Eloise was everything that Ben's family hated. They saw her as an uptight, highbrow, fancy broad who thought she was too good for them, even if she didn't say so. Eloise and Ben seemed to have been brought together by mutual rebellions against their respective families.

The first time Eloise brought Ben home for Sunday dinner—the two of them roaring up the family driveway on a huge Harley-Davidson—she saw her father staring at them through the kitchen window . . . goggle-eyed. Donald was a small, neat, precise man, set in his ways. He knew that he was looking at a young man who might become his son-in-law. Watching Ben putting a huge affectionate arm around Eloise's waist as he helped her off the "bike" and then grabbing her hand possessively as they started toward the house, Donald could feel himself repressing an impulse to shudder. He gazed at Ben in his chinos and checkered shirt with what really could be described as anguish. Everything that characterized Ben—big, loud, brash, and common—was the antithesis of the small, neat, precise, almost fussy Donald.

It was not a meeting made in heaven. Donald challenged Ben from the moment he swaggered in the door, questioning his lack of formal education, his lack of manners, and even his lack of judgment in the selection of his tattoos. KILL FOR JESUS! brought special sarcasm into Donald's voice. It was a miracle Eloise didn't run off to the nearest compliant justice of the peace with Ben before they even sat down to Sunday dinner. Later, when that ghastly family occasion was over and Ben had roared off down the driveway alone, Eloise spoke to her father. It was not actually a conversation. Her father, who prided himself so on being rational and reasonable, began to yell that Ben was surely going to be a disaster as a husband. Her mother, who also prided herself on being rational and reasonable, burst into tears, sobbing out "How could you, Ouisi!?" using Eloise's baby name, which she had come to hate.

While the other five girls watched aghast, there was a roaring argument that quickly flared into a screaming match and ended with Eloise running out of the house and moving in with Ben.

Donald and Doris were hysterical. Their problem seemed overwhelming—but Donald was far too proud to ask for help. He certainly wasn't the sort of man to go to an psychoanalyst, but Doris, who had been in graduate school with Paul, and had come back to her senses more quickly than her husband, managed to persuade him that it might be worth their while to lose an afternoon—it was a one-hour trip for them to come into the city—for a consultation. Donald arrived in a rage. Doris arrived fighting tears. How were they going to make their daughter Eloise understand that her boyfriend was a crude thug who would never amount to anything? What Donald wanted from me was answers! None of this psychobabble stuff! Just answers—straight from the shoulder!

"Tell me what we should do!"

Most people ask the analyst to provide them with answers or solutions, but very few of them mean it. So we avoid answering questions as much as possible. Instead, we asked Donald what he and Doris had attempted in the way of persuading Eloise that Ben was not the man of her dreams. They reported that mostly Donald had shouted at her, and Doris had wept. When that hadn't proved effective, he had raised his voice and yelled even louder. And Doris got angry behind her tears and said so.

Now Eloise was estranged from her family.

It took some time in our offices that afternoon, but finally Donald and Doris were able to acknowledge that the tactics they had been employing were not only not working but were having exactly the opposite effect they'd hoped for. We asked if they would consider an entirely different approach — joining. One of the principal difficulties between generations of people who care about each other is that negative feelings are often expressed in actions rather than in words. Not a good idea ("acting out"), but that's the way it is. Very often, kids express ancient angers in the form of actions that seem to represent "a-thumb-in-yer-eye!" Eloise's choice of Ben looked like exactly that. She was putting it to her father and mother and their dedication to education. Her reward for that action was in their responses. On an unconscious level she *wanted* them to be angry, she *wanted* them to be outraged, she *wanted* them to be frantic. *Joining would deprive her of the satisfaction she was getting*. Taking the fun out of rebellion is a principle way of defeating it. When shouting at them doesn't work, try joining.

With Donald, however, that suggestion did not go down easily.

"Eat crow? I'd rather die!! She has to come straight home — and *then* we'll talk!"

Human responses — but they are not very helpful. It was Doris who came to our rescue — having had some experience over the years in placating Donald. After some calming words from her, Donald was able to listen as we set about explaining the merits of joining. We proposed to Donald and Doris that they set out on a course of appreciating Ben. He was, after all, their daughter's choice and as such was entitled to be welcomed, especially if one of the goals of our work was to avoid a continued estrangement with Eloise. Beyond that, we proposed that Donald and Doris should actively welcome Ben's family and friends, actively try to draw them into the world they had created with their six daughters. And, to make it harder, we proposed that this effort had to be genuine. They had to find qualities in Ben and in his family and friends that they could enjoy. Perhaps they could focus on the idea that being welcoming to Ben and his family and friends was a way of keeping Eloise with them. But they had to find something they could genuinely enjoy so that the sound of Ben's Harley-Davidson roaring up the street and into the driveway would make them feel good. (Perhaps "Hooray. Eloise is coming!")

It was a hard sell. Donald was perfectly willing to invite Ben to his house — but it sounded to us as if it would be through gritted teeth, and his conversation would be larded with sarcasm and dislike. We pointed out that they had raised Eloise to be independent. If she was faced with choosing between her father — who was behaving like an angry, wounded rhinoceros — and the man with whom she was "in love" and with whom she was sleeping, it wasn't going to be much of a choice. On the other hand, if her parents were loving, accepting, and gracious, she would have no complaint with them and it was almost certain that the differences between Ben and her family and between Ben's family and friends and her family and friends would become uncomfortable for her and perhaps for Ben as well.

Donald set about mending fences with Eloise. He managed to get a few minutes with her and apologized profusely for his behavior about Ben. He said simply that he supposed the idea of losing Eloise to another man might have caused his overreactions — and there might have been some truth to that — although clearly it was not the only factor. Donald went on to say that he had a great deal of respect for Eloise, and if she was in love with Ben, then there must be qualities in him that Donald had missed. Eloise softened some. Donald then asked her if she would bring Ben with her to church on Sunday and afterward, if she and Ben felt like it, Donald and Doris would take them all out to the main dining room at the university for Sunday lunch. In Eloise's eyes, the university dining room was a special treat indeed.

During the next few weeks, Donald and Doris began to see qualities in Ben that they did actually admire. He was untutored, it was true, but he was also very bright. He had a fierce independence that was admirable. They began to praise him enthusiastically to his face. And the more they admired him, the more uncomfortable Eloise became. Somehow, he was no longer completely hers; he was becoming "theirs."

Beyond that, her family and his family didn't quite blend together. Ben came by his boisterousness naturally. It was the habit of his family not to talk but to shout. They shouted when they were sitting next to each other. Donald and Doris spoke softly in modulated voices. Ben's family was accustomed to beer and pizza. Doris favored an elegant, low-fat menu. When Eloise saw her mother using her very best Irish lace tablecloth for an evening with Ben's family, it was her turn to shudder.

In due time, the excitement of the relationship was gone; both families were increasingly uncomfortable with the other and were growing increasingly critical of each other, although Donald and Doris kept their criticisms to themselves and piled invitation on top of invitation to Ben's family. Eloise's sisters, on the other hand, were slyly critical, which upset Eloise very much because she longed for the approval of her sisters.

Finally, both Eloise and Ben realized that rebellion was not enough. When the breakup came, it was hardly a surprise to anyone — and there was mutual relief all around.

Joining will help very often in these situations. But what happens when it doesn't work? Well, the obvious result is that at least you will have a better relationship with your kid and your kid's choice than you had before. If that is acceptable to you — if one of your goals was to preserve a relationship with your kid — then that will be okay, a benefit, even. If one of your goals was to disown your kid if joining failed, then you can always do that. It isn't written in granite that you must have relationships with your children when they're grown, but if that happens to be one of your goals, we recommend joining.

Many of these situations are far more complex and far more difficult. Let us pose a question for you. What would you do in the following situation? You're the parents of a boy named John or of his wife, Zelda (your choice). John works for the city as a traffic controller. Off the job, he is a heavy drinker. He might be alcoholic, but that might not be the worst of his problems. John's married with two children, a boy, Herb, age four; and a girl, Noreen, age seven. John's wife, Zelda, is refusing to sleep with him. Zelda is also refusing to work—although they desperately need the money since one income is not enough—because she insists on being a "full-time mother." John suspects Zelda is abusing the children. In John and Zelda's household, there is a crisis every week. The latest family dispute was last night. John stopped off on the way home and had a few drinks with the boys. When he got home, Zelda ridiculed him, and he raised his hand as if to hit her. She grabbed four-year-old Herb and held him up as a shield, screaming for the police at the top of her lungs. John backed away, and she put Herb down. A violent argument followed for the next ten minutes which was interrupted by Noreen informing them that Herb had run away.

That led to a terrifying night—a neighbor had called the police in response to Zelda's screams, and the local church hastily improvised a search group. Little Herb was found two hours later, hiding with the neighbor's dog in his kennel. By that time, John had sobered up and calmed down, and Zelda had regained her self-control. The kids went to sleep in their own beds, and John and Zelda agreed that you (the parents of one of them) could come over to talk to them first thing in the morning.

You arrive. The house is unnaturally calm. Herb has been sent off to kindergarten and Noreen to school. You have a half hour before John needs to leave for work.

What do you do?

You find yourself overwhelmed with impulses. Your first impulses are to be critical. You want to scold John about his drinking; you want to scold Zelda for putting four-year-old Herb in the middle of her fight with John; you want to scold the two them for their lack of self-control and tell them both to grow up and behave as adults. Your second impulse is to offer unsolicited advice. It's time that John faced up to his drinking problem; maybe he should go to AA. And it's time that Zelda faced up to the fact that she's putting an unbearable burden on John by refusing to get a job; Zelda should get off her butt and go to work. You want to offer to take the kids for a few days while they get their act together.

The real question here is not about John and Zelda; it's about *you*. How much self-control do *you* have? Interfering in your kid's situation is a great temptation. The urge to rush in, take control, set everything straight, and be the hero or the heroine, is strong in many of us. (Therapists are not immune from those temptations.) We all know the urge to take sides, to "explain" what is going on ("the trouble with you two is . . . ") to "bad-mouth" the offending partner, to set everybody straight.

Don't. A great many families have ongoing problems because of remarks made in a moment of passion—attacking one of the partners only to see the couple reconcile later. The consequences of things said in these situations can linger on for decades and can certainly contribute to making a bad situation worse. One of the major themes of this book is the need to preserve the family fabric, no matter how ragged it may appear to be. We all need families and relationships with the people we care about and who care about us.

Instead of trying to be the hero or the heroine, consider employing the answer that appears so often in this book. Do nothing. Instead of rushing into action with scolding, blaming, or unsolicited advice, ask first if your kid and his wife would mind talking to you about their situation? One of the best things you could say to John and Zelda might be something like "We get the feeling the two of you are in pain, and we want you know that we're available if you want to talk. Do you think that might be a good idea?"

If they agree—and if you go at it in a low-key, noncritical manner they often will—then you can arrange a time when and a place where you could listen to them. Perhaps John could call in sick or take off a half day from work, and you could talk then and there. Perhaps you could arrange for a babysitter for the next evening after he gets back from work so that you could talk with the two of them later—without the distractions of the children.

When you do have an opportunity to talk to them, the first thing to do is to *button your mouth and use your ears. They* are the ones who need to do the talking.

Sometimes, in the beginning, you need to ask one question—a question that doesn't criticize, doesn't blame ("What we'd like to know is how the two of you got into such a mess?"), and doesn't provide its own answer. The unsolicited-advice questions are especially counterproductive ("How many times do we have to tell you that you need to get some help?"). Instead of giving the right feelings of empathy and support and permission to work out their own answers, it provided the wrong feelings ("We've just been criticized") and a solution which will almost certainly be rejected. The right question will help; the wrong question will almost surely make things worse by generating opposition. Please note that both of the two questions just given above focus on you (and how smart you are) rather than on them.

Try a neutral question, one that shows concern, empathy, and a desire to listen to them. How about: "What's going on?"

That leaves John and Zelda with a sense of control, at least in that one area. That reminds them that you're concerned about them, would like to be helpful, but are wise enough not to rush in with an action but can function in the world of words. The best thing you can do is listen—without taking sides—and then keep on listening. You might be surprised at what you hear. Every time we rush in with a question, we limit what the other person can say. Instead of expressing his or her own thoughts and feelings, the other person is limited to answering our question.

Listen. Resist the impulse to make suggestions unless they are requested. Help John and Zelda identify their own solutions. One of the problems of offering solutions is that if one of you offers the solution *you* own it. It's *your* idea, *your* solution, and to kids who are trying to become adults and manage in the adult world that means going back and doing what they're told and being reduced again to the role of children. They don't want to be children again; they don't want to be told what to do; and very often, they will reject anything you say, no matter how wise. How many times have you told one of your kids to "do this" or "do that" only to see them steadfastly refuse? How many times have you wound up with the feeling that any suggestion from you will almost certainly be the last thing to be accepted before the end of the earth?

On the other hand, it's great if John and Zelda can be led to their own solution. Anything either of them thinks of will be far far more valuable to them because *they* will own it! It will be *their* creature rather than yours! So, of course, what we are suggesting here may be harder for you. Telling people how to straighten up and fly right, ordering them around, is much easier and much more satisfying. Of course, it keeps your children from growing up and becoming self-reliant and self-sufficient. Instead try the techniques we've been suggesting in this chapter—joining, avoiding criticism and blaming, avoiding unsolicited advice, limiting yourself to carefully phrased, neutral questions, and doing a lot of listening. We think you'll like the results.

Now let's look at something more difficult. There are some areas of disagreement about your kid's partner (or possible partner) where the conflict is so intense that it that seems irreconcilable. You are devout Catholics, and your kid's choice is a passionate born-again Baptist; you are Jewish and your kid's choice is Muslim; the list is endless. These are issues—and there are many others of the same nature—that can arouse intense passion.

The first question is what are your goals? What do you want? Some people really seem to want to fight and these situations offer an opportunity to fight indefinitely. Some people are not concerned with preserving family ties. They are ready to kick the offending kid out of the family. If those attitudes represent you, this chapter will be of no interest. The authors of this book believe in loving families and—beyond that—believe that warm family ties are necessary for emotional health. Not always, of course, but we are not writing about those situations.[1]

If you are facing the kind of painful conflict just mentioned above and wish to maintain a relationship with your kid, then we must begin by repeating the two sentences with which we began this chapter: If you have a kid who is willing to be guided by you in his or her selection of a lover or mate, something has gone terribly wrong. And if that sentence has to be explained, something has gone terribly wrong. In other words, if you can force your kid to give up a person you think to be an inappropriate companion, then your kid is still a kid. And that's too bad. That kid should get professional help immediately to help him or her grow up.

The authors of this book believe that it is the responsibility of parents to produce self-reliant, emotionally healthy, independent children who are loving and respectful. Grown kids are supposed to be separate people from their parents. They are expected to have their own thoughts and feelings as separate individuals do. It is also expected that they will be responsive to the loving feelings of their parents and return love and respect. If you have succeeded in raising self-reliant, emotionally healthy, independent children who are loving and respectful to their parents you have accomplished much of which you can be proud. But if, in spite

---

1. There are extreme situations where the unfortunate reality is that the family fabric cannot be preserved. These situations may involve physical abuse, sexual abuse, alcoholism and other substance abuses, serious mental illness, and others. In such situations, after professional counseling, it may be in the best interest of all concerned to break off family ties. But, as noted, these are extreme situations.

of that, perhaps because of that, you're still facing a Catholic–Baptist or Jewish–Muslim-type situation, you still have a painful situation on your hands for which there may be no easy solution.

It is a situation that you've probably brooded over and talked about, and if you'd been able to work out a solution, you wouldn't be reading this. The question is whether the teachings of modern psychoanalysis can be helpful in reducing this kind of painful emotional conflict, which so often feature feelings of betrayal and rejection, and help preserve family ties.

The next case we would like to present to you involved Kathleen and Kevin, proud parents of three strapping sons and a fourth child, a daughter, Siobhan,[2] twenty-five years old, a fine young woman, a teacher, lovely (and possessor of a key to her father's heart), devoted to her four Irish-Catholic grandparents, and known to her family as "a bit headstrong." The troubles began when she "took up" with Bobby, twenty-seven years old, also a teacher, a man who'd had a personal religious experience that brought him back into his family in his senior year of college. During his early college years, he had been estranged from his intensely devoted born-again Baptist family.

As it became evident that Siobhan was growing serious about Bobby and he about her, Kathleen found an opportunity to lay down the law—her law. Any daughter of hers (there was only one) who married outside the Church would no longer be welcome in her home or in her life. To Siobhan, that statement was like a red flag to a bull, and she and Bobby quickly announced wedding plans. Kathleen announced that Bobby was no longer welcome in her house. Siobhan announced that if Bobby was not welcome she was not welcome, and left the house.

That was where we came into it, and we think our work failed. All efforts to persuade Kathleen to sit down with Siobhan in a

---

2. Pronounced "Shivaun."

neutral setting, perhaps in our offices, came to nothing. Not while she was wearing "that man's ring." The question remained: what was the family to do? Kathleen was still adamant. The boys and Siobhan's father were torn. In our offices, Kathleen announced that she would never see her daughter again until she was married "in the eyes of God." The occasion for that remark was a family session involving Kathleen, Kevin, their three sons, and Siobhan. The men in the room had all looked troubled at Kathleen's words, but only Siobhan spoke up.

"If that's what you want, Mom."

It seemed to us that this family was about to splinter. We asked if Kathleen had any objection to talking a little more about her dictum. She said she had no objection. We asked if Kathleen, when she said she would never see Siobhan again unless she married in the Church, had meant that none of Siobhan's brothers were to see her again unless such a wedding took place. There was a long hesitation before Kathleen spoke again. We could almost see her weighing the possibility that, in addition to losing her cherished daughter, she was now running the risk of losing at least two of her sons. Finally she spoke.

"That will be a matter of individual conscience," she pronounced.

We asked, "Does individual conscience extend to Siobhan's father?"

Another long pause. Kevin's expression was one of anguish. Then the answer. "I won't be his conscience for him. He knows right from wrong."

It seemed to us there was just palpable relief on Kevin's face after he heard that.

Siobhan and Bobby's wedding took place. Kathleen did not attend. Kevin attended, standing at the rear of the church and leaving immediately after the ceremony was completed. Siobhan's two oldest brothers attended. The third, Michael, did not.

Siobhan and Bobby's wedding was many years ago. Their

children are growing up. From the day of her wedding to this writing, Siobhan has spoken only once to her mother—the night before Kathleen went into a hospital for surgery (temporarily successful). They have never been in the same room together. Siobhan is close to her two older brothers (whose Catholicism is more liberal than their mother's) and to her father (who simply cannot give her up). They have all met many many times at her house and at the houses of her brothers. Her children are very close to their cousins, but they have never met their maternal grandmother. Siobhan's youngest brother, Michael, is supportive of his mother and does not see or speak to Siobhan. That choice has led to some tensions between him and his two older brothers, but his father and brothers know that he is eager to have information about her.

We have given much thought to that case. As far as we can see, the outcome was a failure in the sense that there were losses all around. At least past of the family has managed to maintain some sort of closeness. Kathleen is dying now, and it is the expectation of all concerned that after her death the family will reunite. But what a tragedy. So many losses, all of which might have been prevented had all the parties involved been able to sit down and talk until they began to see each other's point of view and some compromise, acceptable to all, was achieved. We wouldn't have these feelings of failure if we didn't believe that these problems can be worked out—if people will sit with each other and keep talking.

8

A Care Package for Parents:
The Buddy System

It is curious how the troubles of our grown children can take over our thinking. Many of us find ourselves obsessing about the difficulties in which our grown children find themselves. We worry, fret, stew, and argue with our spouses; we often become depressed and are frequently seized by a compulsion to rush in and rescue — to help or offer advice or scold (almost always the wrong things to do) — and there seems no relief. The kids' problems go on and on, and so does our distress.

Of course, a professional therapist — a psychoanalyst, a psychologist, or a social worker — represents relief from that distress. Despite the fact that most of the readers of this book would go to a doctor if they had a troubling physical illness, very few readers will consult a professional therapist to help them with serious emotional difficulties. The reasons for this we leave to the reader. Whether there is a stigma ("people will think I'm crazy!"), fear of the unknown, fear of the cost, or whatever, most people are reluctant to seek out professional help, even when they know they need it. And it is true that some people would like help but do not have it available in their geographic area.

Well, there is an alternative source of help that is possible and free—even if it is not always easy to establish. There is a technique called the buddy system, which has provided comfort and support, over extended periods of time, to many long-suffering parents, and that's what this brief chapter is about. Some of you may be ahead of us; you've figured out that we're talking here about someone in whom you can confide, someone to whom you can unburden yourself and in so doing find relief. But isn't there a price to pay? Aren't many of us reluctant to talk about things so personal, so intimate, and, for some of us, so filled with shame? Well, there is a price, but it's worth paying, because it helps to talk.

Does it help? Really? Yes, it does. Why? Why does it help to talk? What's the purpose of talking, anyway? Well, one widely held and seemingly obvious explanation is that we talk for the purpose of exchanging information. Psychoanalysis holds that there is another and more important reason for talking. Talking is considered to be an effort to discharge anxiety and replace it with a feeling that everything is under control and that we are all right. In other words, we talk to try to achieve an inner calmness.

All that sounds very simple, but it's not. It's our experience that many people don't know how to talk. Many people seem to have the idea that the only purpose in talking is to exchange information and data. And in the small exchanges of the day (is it going to rain today?), that is certainly true and actually helpful. In the *real* conversations, the ones that deal with the emotional issues with which we all wrestle from time to time, information and data are rarely of substantive help. Many real conversations consist of one person presenting an emotional dilemma—often in the form of dry facts—and the listener responding with dry facts— after which they both feel slightly starved, although sometimes they don't realize it.

Why starved? Because each of them is looking for emotional relief, a step toward inner calmness, and all they get are facts. The presenter is already emotionally upset; the listener, presented with a difficult emotional situation, becomes anxious and, in order to reduce that anxiety, rushes in with practical suggestions, most of which make the presenter feel worse. Does the presenter realize that the search for emotional relief went unanswered? Does the listener realize that all those practical suggestions were of little help? Do they both realize that their conversation was frustrating—or were they so cut off from their feelings that they weren't even aware of their emotional hunger?

A baby knows when it is hungry. When a baby wants to be fed, it fusses or whimpers. If nothing happens, it usually cries, and, if nothing happens then, it howls. Sooner or later, mother appears and nurses the baby or gives it a bottle. But feeding for a baby means more than food. It means being held and being comforted; it means companionship and acceptance.

We, as adults, have the same needs—comfort, companionship, and acceptance—but we, as adults overwhelmed by the demands of work and relationships and coping with a society laced with stress-laden modern technology, often retreat from our own feelings into the never-never land of the intellect, facts, and data and become incapable of even knowing when we are hungry, when we need to be fed. We remain vaguely aware that something is wrong, that we have very uncomfortable feelings inside us. Sometimes we try to deaden those feelings through drinking, drugs, compulsive working, compulsive sexualizing, by exhausting sports—all in an effort to deny the hunger within us. What we really need is to be fed emotionally.

When we talk to a buddy, our goal is to be emotionally fed. To get what we need, therefore, it is important that we share our feelings about the problem we are facing rather than deal with endless amounts of data. It isn't the "he did, she did" or "he said, she said" part of talking that brings relief. It is the "I can't sleep; I wake up at two A.M. trying to figure out what's going to happen" and the buddy's empathic "That sounds awful for you" that bring relief. Empathy is emotional feeding, and it eases anxiety. We *need* empathy, compassion, understanding. We don't really need advice and other comments based on information. However, in all fairness, it must be admitted that we often feel as if we need advice, but take a look. See what your own experience is. Our conviction is that you will find empathy and understanding far more valuable than helpful suggestions.

One final comment on this area: How many of you have noticed that having reality explained to you is almost always irritating? At best, such explanations are irrelevant; at worst, they contain subtle criticisms. The friends or relatives whom we consult and who present us with realistic answers, who often seem to have no end of "helpful solutions," who toss around slogans like "tough love!," who are quick to say "well, what you need to do," are all showering us with criticism. The message we are receiving is that they are smarter and we are dumb, that they can see solutions that we are too blind to notice. Most of us, after those conversations, are frustrated. Talk of that kind is rarely helpful.

When we say that talking helps, we mean that nonjudgmental, noncritical talking about emotions helps, which leads to the idea that it isn't enough to have just anyone listening to you. Rather, you need a particular kind of person to talk to and a particular way of talking. If you're going to get the help you need, there are some special qualities you're going to have to look for in a buddy. You may want to add to this list, but let us present you with five qualities in a buddy that we think are indispensable.

1. Your buddy should be a person who can tolerate your feelings, a person to whom feelings are not frightening.
2. Your buddy should be able to listen to you in a noncritical, nonjudgmental manner.
3. Your buddy should be able to keep what you say in confidence.

4. Your buddy should have a problem of his or her own that is more or less of the same magnitude as yours.
5. Your buddy should like you, and you should like your buddy.

Let's look at those more closely. Many of us grew up in critical households and had our shortcomings pointed out to us so often that we grew accustomed to being treated like slightly retarded pets, loved but not admired. Well, that won't do. Criticism is bad for children, and it is bad for parents. One of the worst culprits is the so-called constructive criticism. There is no such animal. Criticism is criticism, and so is constructive criticism. You don't need it. When you're tortured about your child, having someone point out where you went wrong isn't helpful. More than that, a critical person is not someone to whom you can unburden yourself. Why would you want to?

Blaming doesn't help either. Blaming the child or blaming yourself are both bad medicine.

Why are criticism and blaming so bad for us? Because they increase anxiety, guilt, and depression when our emotional needs are to do just the opposite, to reduce them.

That's why a buddy should be someone who can listen to your feelings, be patient and empathic (which is different from being sympathetic), and who will leave you feeling better after you've talked together. That's a wonderful way of judging what is happening between you and your buddy. Trust your instincts. If you feel *good* after you've talked, you've received affection and understanding. If you feel *bad* after you've talked, you've received something negative. If you can't negotiate a better hearing, shed that person.

Please be aware that there are people in this world who are sneaky with their criticisms. Some people will say all the right things and make all the right noises, but you will still feel rotten after you've talked to them. Again, trust your instincts. You're not getting what you need. Don't talk to that person again about your problems with your kids.

In the same spirit, you must have the feeling that your buddy won't gossip about what you've been saying. What could be more inhibiting than the feeling that your most personal problems are going to become grist for the local gossip mill?

Since most of us have learned by the time that we have grown children that there is no such thing as a free lunch, it is our recommendation—for a buddy system to work over a long period of time—that you and your buddy should be mutually supportive. Half your time should be spent talking to your buddy about your emotional concerns, and half your time should be spent listening to your buddy's emotional concerns. And the way you listen—empathetically, without criticizing, without blaming—will help your buddy understand what it is you want for yourself.

In her marvelous biography of the poet Anne Sexton, Diane Wood Middlebrook describes an arrangement between Sexton and her buddy, the poet Maxine Kumin.

> "Max and I say we love each other like sisters—that's kind of a new category [for me]," Sexton commented. With her blood sisters she experienced *only rivalry*, but with Kumin she knew reciprocity. After Sexton built herself a new study, they both had special phones installed on their desks and used them through the day to check out drafts of poems. "We sometimes connected with a phone call and kept the line open for hours at a stretch," Kumin remembered. "We whistled into the receiver for each other when we were ready to resume."

That kind of safe, loving, sharing relationship isn't easy to find. It may take some effort. You may have to reach out to someone you know only casually—someone your instincts tells you might be a good buddy—but take the chance. It's worth being brave and trying. A buddy can be really helpful, and you might get lucky.

9

If Your Kid Might Be Gay,
Or if You Are

For many parents—and their children—it is the waiting and the uncertainty, the months, the years of fearful wondering, the knowing and the not knowing, that is the most painful. The family torment begins when the child is very little; the pain appears in too many suggestive fragments of behavior; when a little girl ignores her dolls once too often in favor of her brother's erector set; when a little boy is just too comfortable in his sister's Wonder Woman costume.

At these dismaying moments, when doubt first creeps into our consciousness, some parents retreat into denial. We push away what is in front of our eyes. It isn't conclusive; it may mean nothing; we shouldn't jump to conclusions. Our unconscious assists us in rejecting these early signs of homosexuality, and often we persist in not seeing them. We never see anything. Sometimes for years.

Or, if we do notice some disturbing piece of behavior, we make excuses. Maybe she or he is going through a phase. We avoid confrontations and live on hoping it isn't so.

Others of us have an opposite reaction: we rush into action. Something must be done. Right away. We begin strenuous efforts to make a little girl "feminine" or a little boy "masculine." Frilly dresses and dancing classes on one side, compulsory athletics and "manly" activities on the other. Or we take them to therapists. Such efforts are almost invariably futile and usually produce unhappiness all around.

When parents get a feeling they desperately do not want to have about their child, they often think they are recognizing something of which their kid is unaware. But children sense their parents' thoughts and feelings and not infrequently have similar thoughts and feelings of their own. The awful sense that haunts us as parents that there is a clear pattern of inappropriate gender interests is matched by our child's sense that he or she is different from the other kids.

That sense of being different starts early. It is usually noticed by our kids somewhere between the ages of five to seven. When it happens, our children are not unlike their parents. They, too, use denial. They, too, don't talk about it. They, too, pretend they are like the other kids. They join us as parents in not seeing anything or saying anything. Our approval is of utmost importance, and most of them set out to try to be what we want them to be.

Some young men, desperately frightened and unhappy about the sexual difference they sense within themselves, act out in the form of "over-masculinizing." They are the roughest on the playgrounds, the toughest on the athletic fields, and, a little later, the most avid pursuers of sexual conquest, all in desperate efforts to prove to themselves and to us that they are "men." Their sexual experiences may very often end in a vague sense of disappointment, but after each encounter, they comfort themselves with the hope that their next sexual conquest will be fulfilling. Such behavior can persist even into marriage and lead to a moment of special pain for all concerned when, sometimes after many years, the grown man finds himself in the grip of his true sexual feelings and leaves his wife (and, on occasion, children) for a fulfilling homosexual relationship.

Some young girls, living with similar fears, move quickly into early promiscuity, driven by attempts to prove—again, mostly to themselves—that they are female and can behave in a female way. They, too, may find these early heterosexual experiences curiously unsatisfactory but persist in hoping that the inadequacy, which they blame upon themselves, will be solved on some future occasion. Like their male counterparts, they may marry and have children before finding themselves overwhelmed by their true sexual feelings. Again, there may be much pain as marriages are ended. And, again, for them, the rewarding sexual experiences they are seeking may be found in homosexual relationships.

In all the work my wife and I have done with homosexual patients, neither of us has ever met one who elected to be homosexual. Their experience is simply that they had no choice. They are the way they are. Sometimes they wish they were otherwise, but wishing doesn't change things. Asking a homosexual to change his or her sexual feelings—to prefer the opposite sex when it is the same sex that is preferred—is like asking a heterosexual to change his or her sexual feelings—to prefer the same sex when it is the opposite sex that is preferred.[1] Either request seems impossible.

Where does it come from? Why my child? Why?!

We don't know. We do have an idea that roughly 6 percent of

---

1. We recognize that there are young men and young women who go through a homosexual phase in their teenage years or in their twenties and later decide that heterosexuality is their true orientation. Such cases are isolated and few. While it is impossible for many parents not to hope that such might be the case with their kid, it is almost always damaging to everyone concerned when parents hold those wishes too dear, put them into words in the presence of their kids, and otherwise press for a change in sexuality that the overwhelming majority of homosexual children simply cannot make. The damage to the family fabric is grave when parents cannot accept their children's sexuality.

the American population is homosexual, a rather steady 6 percent through time, and it is a rare family that doesn't include homosexuality somewhere. It seems curious that with all our scientific progress, we still cannot explain the reasons for that 6 percent.

One theory argues that homosexuality is the result of a breakdown in nurturing, the fallout from some failure in early parenting. That theory, however, has not held up under close inspection. Social science has not been able to explain homosexuality in terms of any identifiable family situation.

The once widely held view that certain family dynamics in early childhood can turn heterosexual children into homosexual children cannot be demonstrated. Domineering fathers in combination with passive mothers, domineering mothers in combination with passive fathers, single mothers, single fathers, all-female household, all-male households, none of these provides an explanation. Homosexuals do come out of some of these households, but heterosexuals come out as well. And both are the products of more traditional households, in the same proportion.

Another variation on the breakdown-in-nurturing argument is that homosexuality is an illness that can be cured, that it represents a truncated heterosexual desire, that the people who today describe themselves as gay are suffering from a maturational lag that, if removed, would progress into heterosexuality.

That thesis, too, has not stood up to clinical investigation. In 1987, the revised version of the *Diagnostic and Statistical Manual of Mental Disorders* (known as the DSM-III-R), which is the psychiatric/psychological communities' effort to codify mental disorders, finally dropped the classification of homosexuality as an illness, long after the idea itself had been generally repudiated in the medical world.

If homosexuality isn't a product of faulty nurture, can it be the result of nature? Is biology producing a variant? Currently, there is a great deal of scientific work being carried out in search of a genetic cause, a mutated gene or chromosome that changes the unborn child's sexual preference in the womb from heterosexual to homosexual.

The authors of this book believe such a cause will one day be found, that homosexuality is biology. For those with deeply held religious convictions, that would translate into the concept that God makes homosexuals as well as heterosexuals, which is, of course, another way of saying that we are all God's children. "Male and female created He them" suggests to some people that we all have a little of each, or more than a little of each.

Not everyone holds that viewpoint. There are people who feel deeply that homosexuality is a sin, that it is the work of some demonic instinct, and must, in some way, be punished. The authors of this book do not know how to be helpful to people with such views. All we can do to respond to such convictions is to quote one ancient, illiterate homosexual's observation, "God don't make no junk."

In general, it is our experience that anyone staking out the high moral ground—whether the issue is conflict within the family, sexual orientation, or anything else—has very little likelihood of dealing successfully with the problems identified in this book. Feelings of being right about an issue, the need to be right is, in our experience, a road to failure. The constructive resolution of family problems requires patience, a willingness to listen to other people's points of view, an ability to seek out and accept compromise, and, always, that greatest of religious virtues, love.

Even when we possess such abilities, they are not always available to us. Amelia, late forties and distraught, came into our offices fighting tears. She had been referred by another patient, although she was certain there was nothing we could do to help her—what could anyone do? She was so desperate that she was willing to try anything. Her only child, Anthony, her only hope for grandchildren, a bright, handsome, hard-working young man who had many girlfriends while he was in school and lived with several of them, was now planning to leave his job to spend the summer in Provincetown, Rhode Island, and was then planning to relocate to San Francisco.

"I can't breathe," she said, fighting tears, clearly on the edge of hyperventilating.

We asked her to take a few deep breaths and compose herself before attempting to go on with her story. We didn't mind waiting, we explained. Studying Amelia as she struggled to gather some composure, it was apparent that being a mother was Amelia's principal role in life, and at the moment, she had a profound conviction that she had failed. She was profoundly confused, frightened, and unhappy. It took some time before she was able to go on talking.

Anthony was twenty-six and had always been a "good boy," she explained. He lived at home with Amelia and his father, Vincent. He seemed to enjoy his parents' company during the week and had a busy social life on weekends. It was true he didn't bring his girlfriends to the house anymore, but Amelia and Vincent had assumed Anthony simply wanted "his own space." They adored him and would do anything for him.

The news of Anthony's plans to leave for Provincetown and San Francisco, however, suggested a separation for which they were unprepared and inflamed doubts that Amelia and Vincent had been denying for many years—which they never discussed with each other or with Anthony. His proposed relocation terrified them in its implications. Both Provincetown and San Francisco were celebrated for their large homosexual populations. Still, Amelia and Vincent said nothing to each other or to Anthony, and Amelia began to feel crazy with anxiety.

Not only were there troubling questions left from Anthony's childhood, but recently, he had begun to provide his parents with more tangible clues, as well. Over the years, Amelia and Vincent had become increasingly distressed that Anthony never expressed an interest in marriage or children—although they never discussed with him or with each other the implication of that lack of interest—but one evening recently he had left on the kitchen table a matchbook from a well-known homosexual club.

Both Amelia and Vincent had noticed and chosen to deny the message that Anthony was sending with the matchbook. The same was true for the phone calls, which were increasing in frequency, for Anthony from young men with voices that sounded feminine to Amelia and Vincent.

Again, while both of them had become aware of the possible ramifications of such calls, neither had said anything to the other. Nevertheless, a feeling had grown in the household that Anthony was somehow more and more cut off from them. When Amelia had no longer been able to control her doubts and had raised the question to Anthony of her hopes for grandchildren he became "testy."

In our offices, it was easy to like Amelia. She was clearly a nice, hard-working woman now in more pain than she could contain. She was convinced that her son was either homosexual or about to become so, and she wanted help. She wasn't quite sure what sort of help she was seeking—and then she blurted out a question: if the worst was true about Anthony, could we "cure him?"

We avoided that question for the moment and asked questions of our own instead. Why had she come alone? Where was Vincent? Amelia explained that Vincent would never discuss such matters.

One of the most deeply held convictions in the world of psychoanalysis is that talking helps, cures, in fact, and that everything can and should be talked about, provided the setting and the manner of the talking are appropriate. Psychoanalysts listen to people talk and see them getting better. Why they are getting better is not always understood, but the fact that talking helps is demonstrated again and again, hence the deeply felt conviction that the "talking cure" is precisely that.

Here was a family with loving members who were not talking to one another. It went even deeper. Here was a family with great reluctance, a great fear, of putting thoughts and feelings into words. If we were to be of help to them, our principal contribution might be simply to help them talk to one another.

Earlier we used the phrase "provided the setting and the manner of talking are appropriate." The setting needs to be calm and with a minimum of outside stimulation. Heavy metal music on the stereo will not help people talk to one another. A blaring television can be equally counterproductive. If people are in a quiet room—sometimes a therapist's offices may be chosen for such serious conversations—they are able to talk more clearly to one another.

In the same way, the manner of talking is critical. If the purpose of talking is to hurt or to criticize or to blame (see chapter 1), and the conversation will include such gambits as "I'm here to tell you what's wrong with you," it's unlikely that the talking will serve any useful purpose. If there is love, compassion, caring, or concern underlying the talking, then it is almost always helpful.

It should be remembered that while we urge people to express a great many of their thoughts and feelings, *there are some things that should never be said*. We all know what they are. They are the remarks that once spoken leave an injury that will never heal, the remarks that will not be forgotten and often will never be forgiven. The angry comment "You're nothing but a whore!" once spoken can never be retracted, and it will stay with the person to whom it is directed the rest of her or his life, and the relationship between the two people will never be the same.

So talking is urged—in the right environment and in the right way. Angry feelings are encouraged. Venomous attacks are forbidden.

Here, with Amelia, we had a clear problem. In answer to her question, we said that if Anthony was homosexual, it wasn't a condition that could be cured, but we did believe that we might be able to help the family. Would she consider trying to bring Vincent to our offices so they could consult with us as a couple?

Later on, they might like to include Anthony in our work.

After much discussion, Amelia said that she felt better for having spoken with us and would try to persuade Vincent to come in with her. Later that same afternoon, Amelia called for an appointment for herself and Vincent. We arranged to see them the next morning. Vincent proved to be a strong, likable man to whom talking did not come easily. Only after the most cautious and painstaking preparation was it possible to put into words the possibility of Anthony's homosexuality, and then Vincent's only response was, "Well, if that's the way he is, that's the way he is."

Amelia said it was not knowing that was so painful for her.

We wondered aloud why Anthony's mother or father didn't ask about Anthony's sexual orientation. Vincent said nothing; Amelia explained in tones of horror that neither of them could ever do that. Asking was out of the question. We wondered if it would be helpful if they were to bring Anthony with them to our office and attempt to explore the subject in our presence. Amelia thought that was a wonderful idea—still clinging, in spite of our disclaimers, to the hope that if "the worst was true" we would be able to "cure" Anthony. She also was excited at the prospect that we would raise the question. We explained we couldn't ask questions for them, but we thought we might be able to bring out the truth, whatever it was. Amelia agreed to attempt to bring Anthony in to our offices. Vincent said little but seemed willing to follow his wife's lead. Two sad and troubled parents left our offices that evening.

A week later, Vincent and Amelia arrived in what seemed to be cheerful moods. With them was Anthony who proved to be, as they had said, a bright and engaging young man. That moment of arrival was the only part of the session that was cheerful. From there on, it seemed all downhill. We began, rather casually, by asking the family what they would like to talk about. Vincent and Amelia both turned to look at Anthony, who clearly felt under pressure to speak.

Nevertheless, there was a long silence. Anthony then began to talk in halting tones, saying that he loved his parents and hoped they would always love him. Vincent and Amelia, looking anxious, assured him that they would. Anthony went on, saying that he didn't want to hurt them, but he felt it would be better if he told them the truth. Vincent could barely mouth the words, "What truth?"

Anthony looked at the floor and answered, "That I'm gay."

His father closed up like a safe. His mother cried. Anthony then provided a long history of his own sexual doubts, his efforts toward maintaining the appearance of heterosexuality in high school and college, and the fact that he had been dating men for the past five years, giving them female names at home so his parents wouldn't know.

Vincent and Amelia had great difficulty with what their son was telling them. Vincent's way of expressing his reservations was to pull back into himself and look troubled. It was Amelia who asked the questions. "Was Anthony sure?" "Didn't he want children?" "Didn't he want a family?"

Each of those questions was received by Anthony as an attack, and he kept glancing away from his mother to his silent father.

Anthony finally answered that their responses had been what he had been most afraid of, that they would never be able to accept him, that he would lose them. Amelia insisted they only wanted to understand—and then asked again if he couldn't ever imagine himself having a "normal" life. Anthony bridled (it was, after all, another question that he received as an attack) before replying that except for the secrecy into which he felt he had been forced, he felt his life was normal.

Vincent shook his head "no, no, no." Amelia said that to her, having a wife and children were normal. It went on that way for the rest of the session, with Vincent glowering and Amelia asking the same questions over and over again, all of them trying to puzzle out why Anthony couldn't be heterosexual the way his mother and father wanted him to be. Finally Anthony looked at the floor and asked, "Do you want me to move out?"

As therapists, my wife and I understood that question as Anthony's way of saying that his mother's and father's inability to accept his sexual orientation was making him *want* to move out.

His question had the impact he desired. Vincent looked shocked, and Amelia burst into tears. Anthony immediately apologized, admitting that his question had been ingenuous. He knew his parents didn't want him to leave home. He understood perfectly well that what they wanted was for him to give up his homosexuality and become heterosexual, which he could not do. He acknowledged that their insensitivity to his situation was making him so angry that *he* wanted to leave home.

The threat of Anthony's leaving had a temporary beneficial impact. Vincent spoke for what seemed to be the first time, explaining that they were a family, and he wanted them to remain a family. He just didn't understand what was happening. He would do anything, he said, to preserve the family.

Amelia spoke passionately now and in new tones, insisting that she and Vincent both loved Anthony, that she supposed his sexuality was his business and not theirs, and that whatever he did was all right with them.

The difficulty was that the emotions underlying Vincent's words and her words were saying exactly the opposite. The unspoken message from them was still that his sexuality was their business, that they couldn't accept his homosexuality, and that not only what he was doing but his very being was *not* all right with them.

Anthony's threat to leave home had temporarily held the family together, but Vincent was becoming more and more frustrated as the session continued. Apparently, when Amelia and he pointed out that their son's homosexuality was not acceptable, Vincent had expected that Anthony would change or that we would bring about change. The more Anthony stood by his guns, the more agitated Vincent became. Amelia cried and cried again.

All of her questions reiterated the single theme that she simply could not endure the idea that Anthony was homosexual. She said she couldn't use the word "gay."

In the face of his parents' unrelenting resistance to his sexual orientation, Anthony finally announced that he thought he should move out—that evening.

Vincent and Amelia then got frantic.

Now it was Anthony's turn to let his anger show. This was precisely why he had never told them, because he knew they wouldn't accept him.

"You're damn right," exploded his father. "This I will not accept!"

Anthony stormed back. He had known they would treat him this way! How long did he have to go on lying to them?

His mouth opening and closing wordlessly, his face a study in desperation, Vincent turned to us for a solution, obviously hoping that we would, with some last minute miracle, change Anthony for him. That hope—erroneous as it was—gave us the opportunity to try to intervene in a positive way. It was time to end the session, so we suggested that no action be taken by any of them until they had all had a chance to think about what had been said and there had been a good deal more talking. We pointed out that Anthony could always move out, and a postponement of any action while we all explored the situation would cause no great ill.

Vincent, Amelia, and Anthony were still troubled, sad, and angry, but we could feel the relief in the room. None of them wanted the family to break apart. Seizing the opportunity to have talk precede action, we proposed a schedule of six more appointments to explore the situation further and see if something could be worked out that would be comfortable for all of them.

As usually happens when a schedule is proposed, the tension eased. We suggested Vincent, Amelia, and Anthony try to talk to each other about the subject at home, but if any of them arrived at the edge of saying something that could destroy the family fabric, we asked that person not to continue but to bring those feelings into the next family meeting instead.

It had been a tough session. All sorts of feelings that had been lying just under the surface had been unearthed and put into words—anger, sadness, disappointment, frustration—and that was for the good. It was, however, only a beginning. We now arranged to see Vincent and Amelia separately in individual sessions and then have Anthony join them for the next one. That two-session cycle would then be repeated twice. Time and talk, we theorized smugly to ourselves, could be great healers. We neglected to give much thought to how much depended now on the kind of talking that went on at home.

Unfortunately, Amelia and Vincent's response to our recommendations took the form of several evenings spent urging Anthony to go to church, hints that he might try going out with girls, and other efforts to lead him away from his homosexuality. Anthony's explanation that it wasn't a matter of preference or choice but simply the way he was didn't register. When he had told them he knew he would be happier if he were heterosexual—but he wasn't and he couldn't do anything about it—didn't make sense to them.

When Amelia and Vincent arrived for their next appointment, it was quickly apparent nothing constructive had been accomplished in the talks at home. They had both continued to find it impossible to accept Anthony's homosexuality. They kept blaming themselves—it must have been something they did—and agonizing over what their neighbors would think. Amelia reported herself as having difficulty looking at Anthony at home, let alone discussing the situation with him. From time to time, she would say that she truly loved Anthony and would accept him whatever his sexual orientation, but the tears in her eyes revealed her real feelings. She was a long way from being able to love him as he was.

Vincent was equally troubled. With chagrin, he reported himself as having become a bully at home, shouting at his son—as if by raising his voice he could force Anthony to change his sexual orientation. Anthony was his father's son; he shouted back. It was only with the greatest effort that the three of them managed to prevent a family rupture.

We asked Amelia and Vincent how much they actually knew about homosexuality. They explained that it was a distasteful subject about which they had virtually no information other than thinking it the work of the devil. We wondered aloud if they would consider confronting their devil by reading; we knew of many books available on homosexuality. Vincent and Amelia were reluctant, explaining that they weren't great readers.

Our hearts sinking, we raised the possibility of talking to other parents of homosexual children. There were any number of support groups (including Parents of Gays) where they could consult with other parents who, like themselves, had been forced to come to terms with a homosexual child.

Amelia and Vincent shook their collective heads. They certainly wouldn't be comfortable talking to strangers about Anthony. We suggested again that they might feel better if they read some of the material that was available or spoke with other parents who had gone through what they were going through. They were not convinced. Their response was negative. Preoccupied with the pain of never seeing Anthony married, of never having grandchildren, and, sooner or later, of having their neighbors "know," they seemed to find little value in what we were offering.

Nothing we were trying seemed to be working.

The next meeting with the three of them brought the situation to a crisis. Having spent the better part of two weeks facing his parents' unwillingness to accept his sexuality, confronted almost every evening with his mother's tears and his father's impulses to shout, Anthony announced that he had arranged to leave school, get a job at Dunkin Donuts, and live temporarily with one of his friends who had caring parents. He had saved his announcement for our offices so there would be a chance for his parents to air their feelings, if they wished to do so.

Her eyes closed, Amelia slid from her seat onto the floor.

Vincent shouted to Anthony "Now see what you've done!" and leaped up to bend over Amelia.

Anthony rose to his feet, his face contorted, and watched as his mother received some simple first aid and was helped back into her chair.

Then he began to cry as he said in a low voice, "I won't be manipulated. I won't stay in a house where I'm not treated with respect."

Amelia's eyes were open now, and Vincent turned toward Anthony. In some way, as if for the first time, he had their attention.

"You can't accept me the way I am. Come summer, I'll get the hell out of town and not bother you any more. Till then I'll be with friends."

Amelia and Vincent stared at their son. There was no question that he meant what he had said. It was Vincent who broke the silence.

"Now wait a minute. We told these people [he meant my wife and me] that we wouldn't make any decisions without talking with them first . . . "

"YOU DON'T WANT TO TALK! YOU WANT TO SHOUT!" Anthony screamed.

"No, no more. These people [us again] have some books for us to read, and there's a group called Parents of Gays your mother and I want to join . . . "

Perspiration covered Vincent's forehead.

"Yes, yes!" breathed Amelia.

"Why do you want to read a book?" my wife asked.

"Because if we don't learn more about . . . homosexuality . . . Anthony's gonna leave . . . and I don't want that."

"Why don't you want him to leave?" asked my wife.

Being dumb is one of the most valuable tools of any psychoanalyst. A dumb question that will help someone talk can be much more valuable than the wisest comment that leaves the other person with nothing to say. My wife's question started a flow of talk. For a buttoned-up, buttoned-down, reticent man, Vincent poured out a stream of love for his son and pain at the prospect of losing him. Amelia couldn't wait to get into the conversation, echoing Vincent and promising that they would attend the next Parents of Gays meeting that they could find.

It took three more sessions to negotiate the family situation. Ultimately, all agreed that Anthony should live away from home and live his own life in whatever way he chose. But they also agreed that he would live nearby and that there would be weekly telephone contact and visits back and forth.

Amelia and Vincent *did* do the reading we recommended, and they *did* find a support group where they could talk to other parents of homosexual children. They began to understand how little we know about the origins of homosexuality. They realized that they were not alone in their situation, and talking to other parents helped them accept Anthony back into the family. He was, after all, their only child, the little boy they had loved and nurtured for many years and whom they loved. By the time they had finished reading and talking, there no longer was a problem. They weren't happy about how things had worked out; they mourned the grandchildren they would never have, but they realized that they were still a family and that was what they wanted.

Fortunately, they became able to treasure Anthony just the way he was. They actually did much better than parents who, on being told their child is gay, are unable to express their negative feelings. Children can feel the difference between compliant, "being nice" type acceptance from the real acceptance that comes after a well-waged struggle. There are parents who are immediately accepting but who do not get out all their feelings on the subject. These people will unconsciously let their disappointment, fear, anger, come out in acting out. The sort of people who will say "I completely accept you, but please don't bring your 'companion' to our house."

There is another situation that, even when handled with delicacy, compassion, and understanding, is still devastating to a family, and that is when a parent realizes that he or she can no longer remain in a marriage because of his or her homosexuality.

Such a person presented herself in our offices, horrified by the step she was contemplating. Denise was forty-seven, had been married for twenty-seven years, and was the mother of a twenty-six-year-old son and a twenty-four-year-old daughter when she reached the point of not being able to go on. Her secret, as she referred to it, had been tormenting her since she was ten. Behind her, lay years and years of confusion and guilt, none of it ever really talked about.

In recounting her emotional history in our office, she acknowledged that she had developed doubts about her own sexuality about the age of ten. Even then, while in the so-called latency period that precedes puberty, she had become frightened by the intensity of her "crushes" on her girlfriends. She sensed, quite accurately, that her attachment to them was far stronger than their attachment to her, and that was hurtful and frightening.

A little later, during the early part of adolescence, when hormones were being pumped into her system, she found herself even more confused. The other girls seemed obsessed with boys, but she still preferred her girlfriends. Fearful that her true sexual orientation would prove to be homosexual—and that she would be discovered and ostracized—Denise plunged into early sexual relationships with boys, becoming known in her school as a girl who was "boy-crazy."

During the summer between high school and college, however, while on a ten-day vacation in the Caribbean, she did have a brief sexual relationship with another girl, which alarmed her because of its intensity. Ultimately, she dismissed it as an episode of sexual experimentation resulting from too much beer, but the intense feelings aroused on that single evening stayed with her.

College, for Denise, was a whirlwind of promiscuity. Pregnant during her senior year, she married the young man, and, to all appearances, they had the perfect union. Yet, as the years went on, Denise found herself far more involved in her female friendships than with her husband, with whom she found she had little in common.

She also found herself more and more unhappy. Despite the hubbub of children's activities in which she was immersed, she sometimes felt inexorably lonely, and unloved. In her middle thirties, living with two teenage children and a husband preoccupied with his work, she began to be drawn to situations in which she would—by accident, as it were—be in the company of homosexual women. She said to herself that it was "amusing" to go to a gay bar; she began to take an interest in female athletics where some of the players were known to be gay.

Secretly, and with much trepidation, Denise allowed herself to be drawn into a lengthy flirtation with a young woman, Laura, who seemed overwhelmingly attractive to her. In time, Denise and Laura became lovers.

Denise was stunned at the happiness she found in her clandestine relationship with Laura. For the first time in her life, she knew who she was and what she was. There was true joy. The possible consequences of her liaison with Laura, however, were appalling to think about. Her children and her husband were entitled to her love and her loyalty. The idea of disrupting her marriage to answer her own emotional and physical needs was simply unacceptable. Unwilling to even contemplate hurting so many people whom she loved, Denise forced herself to break off with Laura.

Then followed seven years of secret misery. Her depression seemed to deepen every day. During that time, Denise turned to her church and attempted to talk to her pastor, but he had little time for her and could only recommend that she take her doubts to her husband, a suggestion she could not follow. Miserable in her marriage, feeling that every day she was living a lie, she persevered in her role of model wife and mother until one afternoon she found herself standing at an open window on a high floor of a tall building and thinking of suicide.

Depression and guilt and loneliness forced Denise into therapy. Once in our offices, however, she still found it difficult to talk, and talking, we theorized, was the one thing that would help her. We persuaded her to explore that moment when suicide had seemed an acceptable option.

"Window on the fourteenth floor?" we asked.

"It was certainly a way out."

"A way out?"

"—of the pain."

"Pain?"

And then the words came flooding out.

"Years and years and years of pain!"

After a long and anguished exploration of her thoughts, feelings, and motivations, of her struggles, losses, and sadnesses, and of her feelings for Laura, Denise decided to speak to her husband in our offices. That solution was not available to her because he refused to come in. If talking was difficult for her, it was even more difficult for him. Instead, she raised the subject of her sexual doubts at home and not to good effect. The more she wanted to talk, the less he wanted to hear. Her husband refused to consider ending the marriage but wished to continue as they were before. Their grown children were not to know. Other family members were not to know. She was to say nothing to anyone about her dilemma.

Denise moved closer to suicide. She took an overdose of sleeping pills, an action that was more than a gesture or a cry for help. She lingered at the edge of death for forty-eight hours, and her hospitalization lasted several weeks longer. From that point on, her husband's request for further secrecy was no longer an issue.

Denise's twenty-six-year-old son and her twenty-four-year-old daughter were told, as were other family members. There was shock, disbelief, sadness, anger, and, yes, curiosity, all around. It was then that Denise's husband agreed to come in, and we held several family counseling sessions to work out the details of a separation so the impact on the children and the rest of the family could be managed in ways that were best for them.

Ultimately, it was determined that Denise and her husband would live apart. They would, however, work together to be good parents if not husband and wife. Therapy was recommended for their children to help them come to terms with what "the family secret" had done to them and to find ways to establish a healthy relationship with both parents.

10

Serious Illnesses—Including AIDS

Part I: Chronic Illnesses

The good news is that there are chronic diseases that, though serious, are completely manageable. Diabetes, for example, can usually be controlled by medication and changes in diet. If a patient is compliant with medical instructions, he or she can usually—with little change in life-style—live normally, work, play, travel, do his or her thing. The bad news is there are chronic diseases that are debilitating, progressive, and life-style limiting. Patients with severe kidney disease, for example, have to put their dialysis treatments before everything else in their lives.

The parents of Jane, a young psychotherapist, were heartsick that she had to go to her hospital three times a week at four in the morning to get in the hours of dialysis she needed to survive. They were heartsick—but grateful. Jane was able to maintain half of her practice but unable to manage the care of her three-year-old daughter as well. When she became ill, she had just been granted a divorce. Although her relationship with her ex-husband was bitter, she and her "ex" had been in the process of trying to get along well enough to at least be good parents. More about this kettle of fish later.

In this chapter, we are not going to discuss specific illnesses but rather what to do, or not to do, when an adult child develops a chronic and/or a life-threatening disease. Our kid's name in the same sentence with the words "diagnosis," "illness," or "chronic," strikes terror. When we can take a breath, we ask, "how bad, just how chronic," and, "could it kill?" Then, what do we do, where do we go, who helps?

The Best Consumer Is the Informed Consumer

The first thing we and our kid need to do is to take a crash course on everything there is to know about his or her illness. Usually, the doctor will meet with the family as a whole to brief everyone on the nature, possible progression, and prognosis of the illness. Every good doctor, according to Dr. Terry Weill,[1] knows the importance of having everyone who is concerned with the kid's well-being present at this meeting.

Once informed of what to expect of the disease, we need to call Social Security and find out what entitlements are available; we need to learn what our kid's and our insurance policies will pay. It is necessary to find through our doctor, clinic, or hospital a really good medical social worker who can put in place all the services our family will need from financial benefits to, if necessary, home health care.

We will also need to find the organizations that are dealing

---

1. Dr. Weill is a caring psychiatrist with whom we have both worked for years and who has been kind enough to serve as an adviser for this book.

with and advocating for victims of our kid's disease. All ills, such as lupus, cancer, epilepsy, muscular dystrophy, diabetes, and AIDS, etc., have such associations.

Tasks and Considerations Ahead

Our kid is an adult.

As parents of a sick kid, we don't take charge but instead ask "How do we help?" How do we help our grown up son or daughter do what he or she needs to do, get to where should he or she needs to go, and who, besides us, helps?

We listen first to our kid's spouse or significant other — even if divorce has reared its ugly head. We are deeply considerate of our kid's friends and associates.

First, we listen to his or her spouse or significant other. We are not our kid's sole support anymore. We need to make room for everyone in his or her life. As graciously as we would treat friends of a friend of our age, we must treat his or her friends. When our kids were small, we took care of everything, including who their friends were. Now our kid is a grownup who deserves our respect and courtesy to the people he or she has chosen as friends or lovers. Our adult children make their own decisions about their associates, their careers, their friends, and lovers, and also about their health care. We are there with our support. Even if we would make different choices, we must, now that they are grown, support theirs. And folks, that can really be tough if they choose doctors, friends, husbands, or wives we perhaps would not have chosen for them. If their choice is different, we shut mouths, grit teeth out of their sight, and support *them* and *their* choices.

Empower our kid—and also ourselves!

We and the rest of our family need to do everything we can to empower the sick kid. We ask our adult child how much help he or she wants. In most instances, it will be all the support we can give. If that is so, we as parents—together with our kid—need to get a plan into place about who is to do what. Everybody's abilities and resources must be taken into account, as well as everybody's limitations. Here is where we as parents are going to need a very special kind of strength—the guts to know ourselves and just how much we can and cannot do. We must not promise to do more than we're able to do. When we put our heads together with our kids and marshal all the resources—family, friends, and yes, the state—we can create an effective plan of illness management that won't bankrupt any part of our kid's support system financially, physically, or emotionally. This is really tough. We may want to do more than we can. Our kid may want that. It won't work.

Everybody has limits. We can't live forever. If our kid has an illness that will last a lifetime, we will have to make plans for after we are gone. In the immediate future, we are going to have to obtain enough support to carry the burden. We will have to resist the impulse to make our kid into a child again. This will be particularly difficult if our kid wants to be a child again because the illness arouses feelings of being helpless. We and our kid will both need good boundaries[2] in order to successfully navigate the terrain ahead. If possible, we need to let our kid lead the way in teaching the rest of the family the crash course on the disease. Let

---

2. Good boundaries means that we all know we are separate people; as mother and father, we have our own thoughts and feelings, and our kid has his or her own thoughts and feelings. We don't expect our kid to have ours, and our kid doesn't expect us to have his or hers. Another way of describing boundaries is that we respect our kid's autonomy, and our kid respects ours.

our kid call the social workers to help with the questions about insurance, disability, financial options, and, if necessary, legal issues. Get him or her to be the first to join the support associations that provide service and information about the illness, the latest in treatment options and political and community support for those who are ill. We need to help our kid get to know others who suffer from the same disease and who are living with optimal wellness. We will both find enormous reservoirs of experience, strength, and hope as we meet others in our situation who have performed the tasks in front of us.

Commandeer support.

At the onset of the illness, we need to gather everyone who loves us and the kid into a support network. Tasks divided among many are small. Tasks left to one or two are monumental. Big problems broken down to smaller ones, one day at a time, are manageable.

When Jane began dialysis treatment, her mother and Jane's ex-husband were bowed down by Jane's catalog of needs — she had to be taken to the hospital three times a week and then brought home five hours later; child care had to be provided for when she was out of the house. Jane's ex-husband and her mother also had to deal with Jane's father and his "I-know-what's-best-for-my-little-girl-and-I'm-taking-charge" attitude, which usually sent Jane's mother into a helpless depression and triggered headaches and made Jane's ex-husband mutter of "getting a baseball bat."

Papa wouldn't stop ranting and raving, and Jane's mother couldn't stop crying. Jane's ex refused to speak to Papa, and Amanda, Jane's daughter, was having nightmares. A dialysis shuttle was formed. Jane's friends and family members and colleagues all agreed to take her one-way once a month. A schedule was made, and everybody was delighted to have a little one-on-one time with Jane on a trip that was not too hard or time-consuming. Mom and Hubby were grateful for the respite. For others, the task was not too onerous. The care of Jane's daughter was a bigger problem but one that was eventually solved. Papa's intransigence was a harder problem.

We must not let anything get in the way of our family's collective belief in its ability to find solutions to problems and illness management.

This is the time to draw together. This is the time to open our doors to all who love us and our kid and who will help. Some who we think will be a great support won't be, and some quite unexpectedly will be rocks of Gibraltar. Take those who will help gratefully and let those who won't go without acrimony. This is the time to honor our family's deepest beliefs and sources of strength. For some that is religion. For some, it is the still-small voice within themselves. The morning after Jane's mother, Sally Rhodes, got the news her daughter would be on kidney dialysis for the indeterminate future, she found herself sobbing at the kitchen sink. She wasn't a woman used to praying but she did. She just cried, "Help," to the universe. After a bit, as she stood there, she remembered an old story she had read to her kids. *The Doll's House* by Rumer Godden. It was about a two-hundred-year-old tuppence doll carved of wood. In the story, whenever the doll, Toddy, needed strength to face insuperable odds, she would remember the wood she was made of. Laughing ruefully, Sally said to herself, "well, it's time for me to remember the wood I'm made of." She dried her eyes, sat down and called every one in her address book and told them, "The good news is that Jane is a good candidate for a transplant. The bad news is that she has to be on dialysis until we get one."

Then she said to herself, "I hope I'm made of oak" and called her ex-son-in-law and told him what she'd done. She asked him if he would like her to call his and Jane's friends. He was relieved emotionally by not having to "go through the story again" and gratefully, if grudgingly, gave Sally a list to call. He was surprised to hear from Sally but was glad to hear her say, "I know you and Jane are split, but I want to do everything I can to help you and Amanda. Tell me what I can do to make this easier for you."

"Get Jane's dad off my back."

"Dear, I'll try." And hoping she was made of sequoia, Sally got into her car, went to her husband's office, barged into a meeting he was chairing, and said "I must see you now. No, nobody leave."

Sally became a fierce and powerful force straightening out her family. She informed her husband right in front of his colleagues that he was going to stop yelling, stop controlling, stop criticizing, and start treating Jane's ex with the same courtesy he treated his boss. Then she said he could be helpful by taking his grandchild Amanda out every Saturday morning for the near future at least. Also, she informed him that he would be picking up Jane from dialysis every other Thursday. She also said she insisted he see a therapist about his temper if he wanted their marriage to continue. Then she said to his dumbstruck colleagues that she would be calling them for support in taking Jane to and from her treatments. They weren't to worry — they would only have one trip a month. Since Sally had always been such a rabbit heretofore, Jane's father's jaw dropped, and he was as speechless as his colleagues as she left. He made a parting shot, however, that initiated Sally's turning from a fifty-eight-year-old girl into a grownup woman: "Well if you could take charge of anything besides house beautiful, I wouldn't have to take care of EVERYTHING ELSE!"

Sally was smart enough to let that sink in over the next few days as she continued to rally supporters. Offers of help poured in from almost everyone they knew. As Jane's illness progressed ex-hubby, ex-helpless mom, and ex-know-it-all-dad, along with the rest of the extended family, were able to meet Jane's needs. This didn't happen overnight.

Divisive and destructive emotional coalitions can arise in the family, and old and dysfunctional family ways can continue in a magnified state. Everyone can blame each other and generally behave like banshees lacerating each other and making life hell on earth for themselves and the ill person.

In the face of a chronic illness, families often get caught up in blaming each other. Being afraid of the results of the illness, and also of the extra load of work it imposes, can cause real emotional problems or exacerbate ones that were already there in the family before the illness. Sometimes a scapegoat is chosen. Sally was good about Jane's ex and was able to come to a new way of being with her husband, but she was not so great about her other daughter, Nancy, whose career she deplored. Nancy was a stand-up comic, which to Sally seemed like no career at all.

When crisis strikes, another kid in the family can be the designated "bad one" who "doesn't care or hasn't done her share." Bonding can take place between some family members to the exclusion of others. At first, Sally kept Jane's brother Bill informed of every development in Jane's illness but somehow often forgot to call Nancy. It is very natural in a time of illness to want someone to fight with or blame or ignore. In this crisis, we can't afford that kind of emotional immaturity. More than ever, we need to be parents who exhibit adult behavior.

The second time she was hospitalized, Jane herself laid down the law: "If you are going to help me, it has to be all of you according to what is comfortable for you to do. I know Bill was here last time every day and Nancy wasn't. Well, Nancy sent me those cartoons that cracked me up. We all know she can't stand hospitals. Everyone is to be told the same thing at the same time. There will be one consult with me and my doctors, not lots of little gossip sessions. I will decide on my medical treatment, and you guys will back me up. It makes me frightened and miserable when one of you says he does more for me than the others. Please, just all of you don't fight. It makes me sicker. So, dear Mom and brother, get rid of your halos. Dad, talk in a lower tone of voice and take the demon outfits off my sister and ex-husband."

Later that evening, minus Nancy, a number of friends and family sat around Jane's bed listening to a tape Nancy had made for Jane of a poem she had especially written for the occasion. Since Nancy was a very funny stand-up comic, the tape was hilarious and reduced the whole group to paroxysms of giggles. Nancy made many more tapes for Jane that she listened to during her long hours of dialysis.

*We must not try to pretend that things
are the way they were before the illness.
We must, however, lose that
marine-corps-stiff upper lip.*

We will all, at different times or sometimes together, need to grieve for the past. We will need to recognize that we miss life as it was, both the fine and the lousy, that we are frightened, mad, tired, lonely, and hate what the illness is doing to us, our kid, and the rest of the family. Sometimes on a bad day, Jane's mom, Sally, wanted to take to her bed and tell her husband "to handle it." Sometimes Jane's dad got sick of his wife's bloody new assertiveness. Bill missed being his mom's favorite. Nancy missed her role as the "wild" one. Jane would be demanding and petulant, and everybody would miss her being "the good one." And on the fine side, they missed their family's parties, vacations, and blessed physicality and good health.

When mad, we FIGHT.

Not each other but the disease. We volunteer at the organization that supports families like ours and our kid. We do something political. We write the White House. We demonstrate. And sometimes we throw things if we must. We have a right.

When sad, we CRY.

Feelings not expressed will poison our life and our relationships. So we learn not to be afraid of expressing the sadness that we feel. We find a Buddy (see chapter 8). See a therapist. We share our feelings with our spouse and other kids. With our friends and with our kid who is sick. That gives permission for the rest of the family to share how they feel and all will be the better for it.

We don't blame.

Many families go through long periods of blaming themselves for the illness. Weird though it sounds, they have trouble forgiving themselves. It's a kind of survivor guilt. We have to say to ourselves, "Illness, like life, happens." Let's get out of the problem and into the solution, and if there is no solution, at least into the most comfortable endurance possible. The crisis of disease can make us see all our failures writ large because on a very primitive childlike level we have to find a reason for the disease. We have to find a way to deserve what has happened because thinking of

illness as a random tragedy without rhyme or reason is more
chaos than we can stand. When afraid, we want order. Alas, there
is no reason for disease hitting some people and not others. True,
there are behaviors that lead to some ills. And people get sick
and/or die. At the point someone is ill, this kind of ruminating
adds nothing but salt to the wound of the illness. We need, in bad
times, to try to dwell on what is positive about the family — its
strengths and endearing idiosyncrasies. We need to identify our
sources of strength past and strength present. Jane's family always
used to laugh behind their stern and uptight grandmother's back
and mimic her, saying in plummy tones, "We have always func-
tioned in disaster." Jane's mother, Sally, remembered that
particular hard wood "she was made of" as she stood sobbing at
the sink. It helped her to "function in disaster." She got busy calling the names in her address book. She dealt with her former
son-in-law despite the detritus of blame and shame left over from
Jane's and his marriage. Jane needed his support, too. Sally made
it possible for him to give it. That she didn't like him very much
became absolutely immaterial. As they worked together to meet
the child Amanda's needs, she became very fond of him as the
father of her grandchild.

Oddly enough, this family became a closer and stronger family
through pulling together to support Jane and Amanda. Sally, the
mother, grew up. Nancy's career choice as a stand-up comic
became respected by the family. Dad mellowed and became
closer to his family once he realized he didn't have to play the
role of family controller and take total responsibility for the well-
being of the family. Through Sally relying on her husband rather
than on Bill for emotional support, Bill became able to pursue his
own needs more freely. Jane and her ex were able to be excellent
parents to their child as a result of all the family support. Amanda
had the joy of grandparents and an aunt and uncle who really
enjoyed her and loved her as well as her parents. And Jane got to
drop the role of the family's "good one" and on some days be

petulant, demanding, and impossible. Actually, there were days when Jane raged, raged, and raged some more. Being a therapist herself, she knew how important it was for her to have and express all her feelings. She got in touch with a lot of anger that intellectually she knew she had always had about having to be the good child in the family. In her illness, she allowed herself to feel and express the old poisonous emotions and the new anger at being sick and clear them out of her system. The family became pretty good at expressing their feelings and, when necessary for their own comfort, set limits for Jane. She could rail and rage all she wanted, but she couldn't ask for a drink of water six times in a half hour. The family got good at listening to Jane express genuine feelings. They discouraged, however, low-grade whining. Jane was too mature and healthy to use her illness as a crutch or a bludgeon. This can, however, sometimes happen. Families must not be blackmailed by the illness.

When we're the support system, we learn to be selfish.

Dr. Weill says, "Not all patients are Beth in *Little Women*." As we said earlier, we can't deal with a long illness without support. Then, we must become selfish. We have to figure out just how much we can do, give, and, in how much time. We must not promise to do what we can't or won't do. Why be selfish? Because if we don't meet our needs we can't meet anybody else's including our kid's. If we are weak, tired, emotionally and financially drained by trying to do and spend more than our resources can bear, we will be no good for our kid. We can help. We can't do or provide it all. If our finances are limited, we can still be at the hospital negotiating and advocating for our kid. If we've got a lot of money, but not the strength to see our kid in a hospital, we can at least provide the comforts and goodies that make hospital stays bearable. If we don't have money, we can give time at the bedside. Hopefully, we can provide both. We have to provide according to our means and abilities. Nancy's poems meant as much to Jane as her brother Bill's visits. So, we do what we can, even if it is not as much or of the quality we would like. Sally realized that she wasn't able to be Amanda's sole babysitter. She took the child one day a week. Her husband and she together did Saturday. They arranged for a playschool and a babysitter for the other days until Amanda's father came home. Brother Bill and sister Nancy were able to help out, too.

Jane remained on dialysis for eighteen months before a kidney became available. It took a year for the kidney to "take" and for Jane to regain stable health and to fully function as she had before her illness. Luckily for this family, Jane's illness, though an horrendous experience for all concerned, was also a catalyst for wonderful change and growth.

Not all stories end so well.

I pray you don't need to read Part II of this chapter, but if you do, just remember, it ain't over till it's over.

Part II: Illnesses That Are Worse Than Chronic, Like AIDS and Some Cancers

The new and good news about AIDS is that it is no longer an automatic death sentence. Still, it is the worst of illnesses in that it lays its victims open to so many other often fatal ills. Nevertheless, many people with HIV can live productive lives, possibly for decades.

Although I have worked with AIDS patients and their families for the last seven years and stood by many two breaths past death, I find the following almost impossible to write. I used to cry when the birth dates on my clients' charts were the same as my children's. Now, they are often much later than my kids'. What do I mean used to? I still cry when I see a twenty-four-year-old at an intake. I cannot bear to count the numbers I have seen cut down by this plague. It is well into the hundreds. I have seen babies, men, women, children of all ages, all social classes, of all talents, all economic strata, myriad ethnic groups, religions, races cut down by AIDS. I have seen them live with this death sentence diagnosis from three months to twelve years. "If I should die before I wake" is a very real consideration for my clients, their families, and friends. How do you plan for anything if you don't know if you'll be around or not? Actually, none of us know when the dread hour cometh, but we don't think about it and go about our lives as if we'll live to ninety. And we certainly expect that our offspring will outlive us.

I remember the mother younger than myself who kept saying on a ride to Albany, "My son was a gay young man. He was twenty-two. When he was dying I couldn't bear to think of him not having me and food and clean sheets. So I try to help. Other young men. The women. The children. My son was a gay young man. He was twenty-two. My son was a gay young man." She kept repeating it. Later I heard her saying it to officials in the halls of the legislature, to anyone who would listen. It was as if that phrase was a mantra that kept her going. That and her helping. And I have seen mothers who have lost all their children and many of their grandchildren. At a memorial service for her last child, I asked one sixty-five-year-old mother accompanied by two active great-grandchildren how she bore it. "What can I do? I can't help being alive. So I just go on. And little James here is only ten, and Vanessa eight. What can I do?" And then there are the many parents who have said to me, "God won't give us more than we can bear." That one always gets me in its stoic acceptance and courage. I want to yell "God didn't have anything whatsoever to do with this if God is all loving, all powerful." No one on this earth deserves AIDS.

No one deserves AIDS or cancer, just as no one deserves racism, genocide, physical or sexual abuse, neglect, floods, hurricanes, earthquakes. God surely can love and care better than I, a mere mortal, and even I, in my most vengeful thoughts, can't wish AIDS on anyone. Pol Pot or Hitler? Well, I'm talking intellectually, spiritually, and ethically here, not emotionally. When I hear of great evil, cruelty to children, I, like the rest of the human race, feel visceral rage and want to tear the perpetrators limb from limb. I cannot understand a universe that allows it. Suffice it to say I am merely mortal with limited understanding. All I do know is that in my personal belief system the greatest sin is to judge others, and the dictum of Christ's, "what ye do unto the least of my brethren, ye do unto me" is the terrifying watchword of my heart. I'm going on about this because it seems to me that those who judge and condemn people with AIDS have turned away from the good, the passionate, all-powerful flow of love that I call God, Christ, and some call Allah, Buddha, Krishna, Yahweh.

The best we can say about prognoses for AIDS now is that hopefully it is turning into a chronic illness rather than one that was sooner or later always fatal. We have new drugs—the protease inhibitors. We don't know how long they will work or what side effects they may have as time goes along. The drugs are very difficult to take because they require very strict regimens. The patient is deluged with planning when to eat and when not to eat, what to eat and at what time, with so many hours this way and that way between doses. The drugs often cause extremely uncomfortable side effects until the patient's system has adjusted to them. The good side is that we see people who suffered dementia, wasting, and ever increasing infections, who were near death, transformed. They have clear heads, excellent weight gain, and return of energy. Infections stop and don't return. To all intents and purposes, they look and feel in good health. How long this will last, we don't know. Believe me, not all of them are going to be able to return to the same activities and work schedules they shouldered before. But some, with support, will be able to as long as the new medications work.

To maintain wellness, the person living with AIDS needs, as well as high-tech, up-to-the-minute Western medicine, stress reduction treatments, and Eastern medicine techniques. Consequently at Village Center for Care AIDS Day Treatment (VCC) where I work, we provide talk therapy, accupuncture, herbs, chiropractic, psychiatric treatment, massage, support groups, and help with concrete services and negotiating the entitlement system. Nobody can afford AIDS. All need financial assistance, which comes mostly through Social Security for the disabled. PWAs (persons with AIDS) also need legal services to help them provide for children who they may be leaving behind who may or may not be HIV positive themselves. They also need support from family and friends, elected officials, and the kindly citizenry of our country since there are so many groups in our society who do not think the Golden Rule applies to people with AIDS.

Of course, every day, we keep praying for a vaccine, for a cure. The hope is that HIV and AIDS will become manageable like most diabetes. For the best advice I know of on handling AIDS I suggest you read *When Someone You Know Has AIDS*, by Leonard J. Martelli, Fran D. Peltz, William Messina, and Steven Petrow. Mr. Messina is the director of VCC Aids Day Treatment. He is one of the finest clinicians we know and has been fighting the AIDS battle since there were only 1,100 known cases. He has lost his life partner and innumerable friends and colleagues, as well as clients. But he never stops fighting. Quietly, steadily without *Sturm und Drang*. Day after day, year after year, he chips away at the power of AIDS. Uncanny, innovative, homespun as well as high-tech medical and psychological smarts are the shores of his practice that first and foremost is a powerful river of compassion, empathy, and respect. He is a man who holds all people equally dear. He doesn't try to do this. Despite what may be considered my hyperbole, he is no plaster saint. It's just the way he is.

Drag queens and crabs, stars, and STARS are of equal interest to him; druggies and presidents of companies, Yonkers Haddassah housewives and feminist nurses, clients and staffs, schizophrenics and moviemakers do not exist in a hierarchy for him. He treats his fellow human beings as though they all stand in a circle rather than on a stair. His book on how to care for someone with AIDS is the best guide I know to helping anyone with a longterm illness. Unfortunately, it was written before the new medications. He needs to revise it now that AIDS is more a chronic than a fatal illness. Still, as it is, it will help you more than anything I can think of with the very down-to-earth problems of caring for someone who is dangerously ill for a long time and steadily deteriorating. If this describes your situation, run, don't walk to your nearest bookstore.

The stuff in Bill Messina's book

It is very important that we plan for the future. Bill shows us how. We must face the facts about our kid's disease, the possibility of cure, or prognosis of death. Bill's book offers a blueprint of how to plan for legal issues and suggests how to provide for our kid's children if there is no other parent prepared to take them and we have to plan for their future. He writes of the perils of foster care and suggests ways that, if we can't take them ourselves, we can find the appropriate person in our family network or our child's network of friends who can. Somebody will need to be appointed a guardian if our kid is incapacitated. We need to get some legal advice and help from a social worker and lawyer on this *before* the problem needs to be addressed. Our kid needs to have a health care proxy and living will to insure that his medical wishes will be complied with if he should be unable to make his wishes known. He must decide who should have his power of attorney if he is *non compos mentis*. Bill's book deals with the above issues at length and with our relations with our kid's social network and how all who love our kid can work together to help him. Bill also has excellent suggestions on how we can help ourselves and very practical advice on how we handle the increasing severity of the illness until the end.

PART III: Dying

Sometimes, even if we can't be cured, we can be healed.

The last tasks of life.

For many, the developmental stage of dying can be the most important, the most dynamic, the true pinnacle of their lives. I have seen these individuals and their families live, not just die, their deaths and accomplish the tasks of the dying stage with luminous grace and courage. These are the people who are able, after great struggle, terror, despair, and the concomitant work, to face the end of existence as we know it, to become as the Episcopal prayer book says "no more seen." What happens after death no one truly knows. That's why I like the Anglican phrase, "to be no more seen." That indeed is all we have proof of about the after-life. These people review their lives, come to terms with what they have done and left undone. They make their amends. They manage to straighten out their relationships. They manage to clean their mortal house of hate, pain, and sorrow; they learn how to say goodbye, farewell. Before the last physical deterioration, they wrestle and put to rest the issues of their lives—whether it be addiction, failures of love, crimes, painful relationships, or the always profound mourning for the future that will not be. Family, friends, doctors, nurses, priests, social workers, and therapists can and do play a dynamic part in helping the dying person to nego-tiate these last tasks of living. They do so by coming to terms with their own terror, rage, and helplessness in the face of death, so they can be there for the dying. Because, after all is said and done, medically, emotionally, and spiritually, all we can do for the dying is to see that they have a clean bed, are kept out of pain, and are not alone. All we can do is be there, or in the next room. That's it. It's some job, parents. I pray that if you have to face it you will be given the grace and strength to bear it.

Thanks to Kubler-Ross the emotional stages of dying are well documented. She found the paradigm for the universal stages that happen to people who are faced with terminal illness. Their loved ones go through the same process as the patient. Sasha's boss, Bill Messina, gives the best description of these stages and so we quote him here:

> Of course such stages overlap, and people may move from one stage to another and then back again. Not all people will go through all stages. Certainly no one *has* to . . . Remember, too, that these stages are very similar to what *you* may be going through as you face the approaching loss of your friend [i.e., child]. The stages are denial and isolation, anger, bargaining, depression and acceptance. What follows is a brief description of each, how you can help your friend [i.e., child] through each stage, and how the knowledge of the stages can help you."

We will now discuss these stages in terms of parents and adult children rather than of spouses and friends as Bill does.

Denial

Thank God for it. It protects us from going crazy until we can bear the truth. At first the diagnosis of any life-threatening disease will elicit this defense. We do not try to get our kids out of denial unless they are in enormous physical or emotional pain or making decisions that could hurt their well-being. This is the time we will all be running around getting second medical opinions, telling ourselves we will beat the sickness. And some of us may just stay in denial. And that's okay. It's the way many people cope with death.

Anger

This is the why-is-this-happening-to-us stage. We and our kid will strike out at anyone or anything within our range, especially those we love the most. We will lash out at the medical profession. We may try to hurt everyone who is standing by us simply because they are there. We ask them to have patience. We tell them that if our anger is too much for them, we'll take it somewhere else till they can stand it again. We and our kid need to be allowed our anger. We have a right to our anger. The thought of losing someone we love so much spearheads our rage and our fear. There is no answer. Nevertheless we and our kid need to express our feelings to each other, to a therapist, to a buddy, a group or any one who will listen. Don't shorten this stage for yourself or your kid. As the Welsh poet Dylan Thomas said, "Do not go gentle into that good night." Now is definitely the time to "rage against the dying of the light."

Bargaining

At this stage we bargain—if I get well, if my kid gets well, I will take care of the sick for the rest of my life. Let him just live till Christmas. I will eat vitamins and seaweed six times a day and never under-tip again, and he will make it till June—no bargain is too far-fetched. It is the stage where our denial and anger break down and we begin to let in the inevitable. You and your kid may achieve some peace at this point. It's a good time to enjoy together and a time to let your kid bring up the problems and issues he wants to solve.

Depression

When we know our kid is dying, and he or she knows it, too, we quite naturally become terribly depressed. We are overcome with grief at our impending loss of our kid. We must stay strong for our kid though because he is losing everything — his very body, his five senses, his relationships, everyone and everything he loves. He is losing hope, future, us, his kids, his dreams, his career, life — simply everything while you, terrible as it is, are just losing him. He fears what will happen to those he loves when he is gone. So, at this stage, we allow our kid to be sad. We don't try to cheer him up. We hold his hand. We have visitors if he wants them and vice versa. If he wants us to go, we go, and vice versa. We tell him how much we love him, that we understand how he feels. We do not monopolize him. We welcome everyone who loves him. That's the job of parents. To make room for everybody. All that we have written in this book about getting support for ourselves and caring for our own needs is trebly applicable here.

Acceptance

To me, death is a lot like birth. The dying person is in labor. All who attend him are midwives if you will. Only we are not helping our kid deliver a baby. We are standing by while he delivers himself to the end of all we know to the beginning of what we don't know. Healthcare workers are divided in their beliefs of what happens when we die. Many are agnostics. Many are garden-variety atheists secure in their belief that this is it. Others have deep and abiding beliefs in an afterlife, and feel they have hard proof of it.

All I know from my work with the dying is Hamlet's speech, "There are more things in heaven and earth, Horatio, than are dreamt of in your philosophy," and I bow to the dictum of a Hindu teacher who said one should not teach spiritual things one has not experienced. So I will not repeat here things I have heard of but not seen. What I have experienced is this. Touching a dying person feels like touching a small electrical charge. A hospice nurse said to me when I asked her about it, "Oh, yes, that's the soul beginning to slip out." Where that electrical something, that soul, that which was our beloved person goes, I don't know. I surmise that if something goes, it must go somewhere "to be no more seen."

During the acceptance stage, before the crisis of actually dying, many wonderful things can happen. This is the time when the patient is more at peace, calmer, moving inward to what is going on inside himself. Be there with him if you can. Pray, sing, talk, be silent—whatever feels right.

As death approaches

The first and most important thing is to see that our child is kept out of pain. There is no dignity in pain. It is unconscionable to allow someone to suffer. Pain can be managed. Your doctor and nurses will know how. In the old days, people were not given enough medications to be comfortable because it was feared they might become addicts. Also there were some sadistic folk about who thought suffering was good for people. Maybe they secretly doubted there was a hell and wanted to make sure people suffered good and hard here before they died. Death used to be in the closet. People died alone in a back ward while their families waited in hospital waiting rooms. For the most part, medical care is much more compassionate these days. If it isn't where you are, get your child to some place where it is. If you and your child wish, get a hospice to provide care for him at home.

We all somehow know when death is coming, even if only unconsciously. This is the time to ask your kid who he wants you to call. Ask him whom he wants to be there. He will know what you're talking about. Sometimes the dying need for us to let them go. We need to tell them it's all right. That we'll be all right. At the last when I held Ray-Ray I told him going was like a featherbed. That he was in a featherbed here, in a featherbed there. It was okay to let go, to sink into the feathers that were both there and here. This seemed to help him loosen the ties of his being to his flesh and later in the night the Is-ness of Ray-Ray slipped out. His face in death was as sweet as that of a sleeping child in a 1920s story book.

At this time, it is very important to perform the religious rites our family may wish. It is very important to say goodbye. We have to do the tasks around death right because there will never be another chance to perform these tasks for this kid again. Thank God. The only good thing about death is that it only happens once to each person.

And here's an antithetical bit: It may be that we may not be able to stand seeing our kid die. That's okay, too. We do what we can. If we have to, we run. Someone will be there if we can't.

The grieving process

It takes a long time. One day at a time, it gets to be five years later. Even then, a sudden memory, a smell in a place where we once were with our child can make us faint. If we have pretty much finished our business with our loved one, we will mourn, and we will grieve. But the feelings will run clean, like fresh blood, fresh water. If we have a lot of unresolved issues we will, as Dr. Freud has taught, suffer from melancholia, that is deep depression. Our feelings of grief will be entangled with congealed messes of guilt, anger, and fear. Expressing them will be difficult. Identifying them will be like trying to see pebbles at the bottom of a stirred up, muddy pond. We can get sick ourselves, suffer panic attacks, have strange aches and pains, even phobias.

If so, we need to consult a therapist and join a bereavement group immediately to help us work through the detritus of conflicting ideas and experiences concerning our kid who has died. We may have handled our rage at his or her getting sick in the first place, have even refused to admit it to ourselves, but might find now that it is boiling up in a bad case of shingles, or arthritis. Even if we've handled everything as well as possible up through the death, we need care and treatment for ourselves. Let's get it so we can go on living a productive life in which we perhaps battle the disease that killed our kid. Yes, one day it will be five years later. We will still hurt. Nothing will have replaced our kid. Still it will be better if we can look back and say we lived and did something useful over those five years and did not just sit, useless in our beds, sobbing and sighing.

Remember Jane? Remember her grandmother with the plummy voice? The old trout didn't have it all wrong when she exhorted those around her to "function in disaster."

11

When You Sell Used Cars and Your Kid Runs IBM—When You Are a Corporate Lawyer and Your Kid is a Carpenter

In 1791, Franz Josef Haydn wrote his "Surprise Symphony," in which more was presented to the audience (primarily his patron, Prince Esterhazy) than met the ear and eye. This will be our "surprise chapter," in which, hopefully, you (as our patrons) will find there has been more included than meets your eye during the initial reading.

One of the most primal fears that affects us all is that of abandonment. It is so basic a fear, so universal that we can use the word "all." Psychologists believe it goes back to the fear that every baby experiences when his or her mother leaves the room, to that early infantile apprehension that she will never return, abandoning the baby to some catastrophic end. Whatever its origin, the fear of abandonment is deep-rooted and pervasive, and it drives us to behavior that we often regret.

Some of us had mothers who were sensitive to our early fears of abandonment and responded in the way we wanted, cuddling us, reassuring us, giving us the feeling that we were safe with them—

which means that some of us, as adults, suffer from the fear of abandonment only a little.

Most of us had mothers who were at times too busy, too preoccupied, too overwhelmed by all the things with which they had to cope. Those mothers weren't able to attend successfully to our baby fears, and our fears of abandonment remain with us to this day. Of course, we usually hide our terror of abandonment. We pose as self-assured. We play mother-of-the-world or dad-who-can-do-everything. Sometimes, we even deceive ourselves into thinking that we are self-sufficient people, which we may be, to some degree. Underneath—in many of us—there is, however, the lurking fear that the people whom we most love, the people on whom we most depend, will go away and not come back.

One of the situations that makes us painfully aware of that special vulnerability is when our grown children begin to lead lives curiously unlike our own. They seem to reject many of our beliefs, some of which we hold sacred— religion, politics, everything we believe in. They live in sin, show no thought for the future, neglect their health insurance, abuse alcohol and drugs, join cults, take up motorcycle racing, or decide to live without doing anything at all, which is especially galling to hard-working parents who value honest labor above almost everything else. Some of them take up work that is wildly at variance with our own. We are management, and they become blue collar; we are labor, and they become management. All of those choices can threaten us with feelings of rejection, abandonment, and loss.

It almost doesn't matter why our children are making choices that give us so much pain. Some of this behavior can be traced to adolescence revisited or finally experienced; other behavior seems to have no rational explanation, but it is there, nevertheless, for us to deal with to a greater or lesser degree.

Let's take a brief look at some of the behavior that causes so much trouble in our personal relationships with our kids. One psychoanalytic theory holds that the fear of abandonment many of us experience is very often an *unconscious* fear. That is to say, it is in the unconscious part of our minds, and we do not realize it is there. That's why that part of the mind is called the *unconscious*, because we are unaware of it.[1] But when there are powerful fears of abandonment lurking below the level of our awareness, those lurking fears can cause us to go into action. We may "act out," which means we may express feelings in action rather than in words—and acting out is very often not in our own best self interest. We may become outraged at something our grown child has done or proposes to do. We may rant and rave about medical insurance, that motorcycle, that boy or girl. When that starts, we're in trouble because we're arguing about the wrong thing. We are really upset about abandonment, but we are arguing about medical insurance, a motorcycle, or someone we regard as an unsuitable partner, which means that the argument never gets anywhere.

It is our experience that most people will reject the ideas proposed in that paragraph—that we have an unconscious mind as well as a conscious mind and that we act out unconscious feelings without being aware we are doing so. Most people will insist that they are reasonable, rational people and that what they are saying is right. We would like to invite you to consider the possibility that both are true, that you as parents in conflict with your kids will be right in your assessment that (1) medical insurance is important to have; (2) that riding a motorcycle is dangerous; and (3) that the boy/girl isn't the person you feel would be right for your grown kid. We also invite you to consider that some of the feelings that underlie your words are based on unconscious

---

1. To "act out" is to express an emotion—such as the fear of abandonment—in an action rather than in words. If I ban my daughter's boyfriend from the house because I am afraid she will run off with him—and, of course, leave me, which is where the unconscious fear of abandonment comes into it, then I am acting out. Oh, I may kid myself into thinking that I am doing it for *her* good, but actually I am doing it for my own. I must learn my own lesson of talking about feelings rather than acting on them. Talking to my daughter and her boyfriend will serve me much better than trying to banish him.

fears—that lack of medical insurance could prevent your kid from getting the proper medical care and he/she will die, that he/she will be killed on that motorcycle, that he/she will be carried away to another state by that inappropriate partner.

It is our conviction that everything we say is a blend of the rational part of our mind (the conscious part) and the irrational (the unconscious part). Everything our kids say to us is made up of the same combination of conscious and unconscious.

Why does this matter? It matters because our relationships with our kids will improve the moment we realize how difficult it is for us as human beings—driven as we all are by unconscious forces like the fear of abandonment—to maintain any personal relationship, let alone a relationship with a grown child who has the power to hurt us so much.

How can we control unconscious impulses when we're unaware of those impulses? Well, one answer to that is that we have to learn how to access our own unconscious mind. The best way we have to do that is to talk and talk and talk (see chapter 9 on the Buddy System) and listen to our own voice and try to hear beyond what we are saying. Behind the words there will be feelings. Ask the obvious questions: what am I feeling? Why am I feeling that way? When did I feel this way before? When will I feel this way again? And listen to your own answers. You can even ask your unconscious a direction question: "Unconscious, why am I so #?*\ mad?"

Then wait. Don't expect an answer right away. It's called the unconscious mind because we can't access it easily. Sometimes—when we're walking, driving, taking a bath—the answer to that question will pop into our head. When it does, pay attention, because you will learn more about the unconscious forces that are driving your behavior.

When we accept that the unconscious impulses within us make it awfully hard to deal with the feelings aroused by these children who turn away from us and cause us such pain, *then* we can have a go at making things better because we can talk, argue, or fight about the *real* issue (our own unconscious fears of abandonment) rather than confusing everyone with substitute issues (the health insurance, the motorcycle, the choice of a companion).

Having opened up our conscious mind to the existence of the unconscious mind, we can then set about trying to make things better. The first thing to recognize is that we are not powerless in these situations. We may, indeed, feel powerless, but the fact is that we are not. When we were babies and our mothers left the room, we were helpless. But we are no longer babies. We are not leaves floating down the middle of a stream, carried any which way by the current. We have arms and legs. We can kick, paddle, and steer. So the question becomes: what can we do on our own behalf?

Let's start by considering Gregory and his wife, Susie. Greg sells used cars on the main road leading out of the small northern New Jersey city where they live. Susie is a waitress. Together they earn enough to manage. They've raised two boys and two girls—somehow—never finding it easy but very happy with their kids. All in all, it's been a good life. Both girls are married and have kids of their own. The older girl is married to a truck driver with a steady job; the younger girl is married to a beer salesman who does very well. Like their mother, both girls have worked as waitresses when they needed extra money. Both of the boys are also working and doing well. Greg and Susie's firstborn son, Tom, is a cop. To the outside world, it looks as if the family is doing well. The trouble is that to Greg and Susie, their youngest kid, Philip, is doing too well.

Greg and Susie adore their kids, and their whole life is built around holidays and family get-togethers. Their dreams don't go much beyond a big, warm, extended family and grandchildren. Underlying their dreams is the wish not to be abandoned, and in order to not be abandoned, they want their children to be pretty much like them and not stray. Like many parents, they want to train their children to be close and stay close.

The Japanese do the same thing with a small potted plant, the bonsai tree. They attach copper wires to its limbs and force them to grow out of their normal patterns into bizarre and curiously attractive shapes. The bonsai tree is a much-admired and loved wonder in the world of horticulture.

Philip is much admired and loved by his parents, but in the last few years, they've become increasingly restless about him. Now, neither Greg nor Susie is much of a talker. Neither of them is very introspective, and they haven't had much to say on the subject of feelings; Greg prefers talking about sports, and Susie is down-to-earth, practical, and so is her conversation. The time did come when they found themselves talking about feelings; and more and more, they were complaining to each other about the feelings aroused in them by Philip.

The germ of it all—almost unnoticed—started in high school when Philip discovered he had a gift for debating. Greg, Susie, and his sisters and brother didn't know what to think. Baseball, sure. Basketball, great. But debating? Philip was unruffled. Words had always come easily to him; he'd seldom been at a loss for the right responses. During his high school years, while his family looked on in some astonishment, he led his high school debating team to a city debating title and eventually to the state championships. The family got their act together and went to the finals in Trenton. They were ecstatic when his team won, but Greg and Susie were less ecstatic when they realized that Philip had won a four-year university scholarship.

Philip's brother and his sisters had gone to the local community college. That had been good enough for them. Now Philip was going away to a four-year program. It was different. None of them had ever done anything like that before. They were proud of him, but there was something in it they didn't like. Philip was so excited—and so clearly wanted to be praised by them—that they rallied around to offer congratulations.

Later, Greg and Susie came to see that scholarship as the beginning of the division between them and their son. Philip thrived at college. It was true that he changed the way he dressed and became a little "preppy," but he was so happy that they couldn't complain. All they knew was that, very slowly, he was becoming less and less like them. Whatever reservations they might have felt, Philip was finding his own way. Not only was he quickly established on the debate team, but he was well-liked and often voted into president of this or captain of that. And, of course, he was debating on a national level and doing well.

When Philip graduated from college, he was quickly recruited by a pharmaceutical company. With his gift of gab and quick mind, he was a natural salesman and soon moved on to be a supervisor of the sales staff. A supervisor! Shockwaves went through the family. Greg and Susie realized that, almost effortlessly, Philip had moved into *management*. It felt like a betrayal. When Philip came to tell them about his promotion—straight from the office and still wearing a jacket and tie—there was a curious lack of enthusiasm at home. Greg got very busy working on the car, and Susie busied herself in the kitchen. The atmosphere was tense, and it stayed that way, although nothing was said.

Philip went hand over hand up the company ladder. At first, his debating skills served him well. In addition to being an outstanding salesman, he became an unofficial company spokesman, being called upon to make speeches or public presentations. Sure enough, he soon became the youngest vice president in the company—which was really a blow to Greg and Susie. Family tensions began to show when he stopped by his folks' house on his way to the annual company Christmas party wearing evening clothes:

"A tux!!" His mother's tone was distinctly disdainful.

"Looks like a head waiter to me!" offered one of his sisters.

"You part of a wedding?" was his father's question.

That time Philip's feelings got hurt. He'd been aware for a long time that there was a singular lack of enthusiasm over his progress up the corporate ladder. When he reported making a big speech and how well it was received, there wasn't much reaction. When his brother, Tom, bowled 272, the fuss the family made could be heard in the next county. Now Philip had really wanted his mom and dad to admire him in his expensive new dinner jacket—and instead they hurt his feelings. When he headed off to the company party, he was feeling lousy.

From that day forward, the family situation deteriorated. Philip began to spend more time with a new set of friends, many of them from the company. He married Jill, daughter of the company's treasurer and a principal stockholder. Greg and Susie went to the wedding but kept to themselves. Jill was pretty and nice, all smiles and cashmere and pearls. Susie didn't believe any of that niceness was real. She'd never had a cashmere sweater in her entire life! Jill didn't seem to notice her mother-in-law's reservations and went on being sweet to everyone, and the sweeter she became, the less Susie trusted her.

Greg and Susie thought Jill looked down on them. Jill, whose mother had died when she was four, was very open to Susie, who interpreted that openness not as that of a girl who needed a mother but as condescension. That didn't make things any better between Philip and his family.

Once the family situation started going downhill, it really picked up speed.

Greg and Susie began to feel that their son had been taken over by Jill's family. Certainly, he had a new set of friends, and it wasn't long before he and Jill bought a new house that was much grander than their own. The down payment came from Jill's father, which was salt in the wound. And Philip was playing golf!

By this time, both Greg and Susie were feeling abandoned. As a result, both of them were acting out. When they saw Philip and Jill, there was coolness in Greg and a chip on Susie's shoulder. There were numerous small disagreements about trivial things, each of which left Greg and Susie feeling worse. So many things that Philip did made them feel that he was moving away from them. Their only response when feeling abandoned was to attack him. Philip then, in turn, felt increasingly rejected by his family. He didn't want to lose them—actually he loved them—but each new accomplishment, including his marriage to Jill, seemed to him to be greeted by further distance from his parents. Finally, there was an explosion, and Philip did attack them, accusing his parents of being unkind to Jill! He cited chapter and verse (and was usually right, if exaggerating things), and the result was a real break. For all practical purposes, Philip wasn't talking to either his father or his mother.

Greg and Susie were distraught. They had never imagined such trouble could happen to them—and it had! Philip was in a rage, and Jill felt terrible, blaming herself for everything, which didn't help.

But some good angel sent Susie to get her hair done.

Sitting in the beauty parlor, she heard a voice from the next chair discussing a problem almost identical with her own except that the speaker (who was a patient of ours) seemed to have received some help. Susie introduced herself and was told that the speaker had solved a very similar family situation with some help from a psychoanalyst. She was even given a piece of paper with a name and a phone number on it—in New York City! That was terrifying! And alien! A psychoanalyst!? If she brought up such an idea to Greg, he'd think she was crazy!

After Philip and Jill didn't even come by the house on Thanksgiving—because they were going to *her* parents' house—Susie poured out to Greg all that she had been told in the beauty parlor, including what seemed to be a guarantee that Sasha and I would be able to restore things to rights. Greg made the phone call, which was the hardest part of it. He was received pleasantly (by Sasha) and taken seriously.

When they came in, they both seemed to be wondering why they were in our offices. Surely their difficulties weren't worthy of our time, and they had made a mistake. (Sasha had suggested to me that we might see them together, so there were four of us in the room.) We immediately agreed that they could very well have made a mistake and suggested that since they were in our offices, it wouldn't hurt to tell us what had prompted Greg to make that first phone call.

Sasha remembered that Greg had said something about difficulties with their younger son. Her memory of what had been said on the phone opened the floodgates, and the story poured out. What wasn't clear, however, was what they wanted from us. Clearly they were unhappy at what they felt was the loss of their son. Clearly they were unhappy at the presence in the family of what they felt was a condescending daughter-in-law. Clearly they were unhappy because of the way things had changed. But what did they want?

At first blush, it appeared that they both wanted Philip changed back to the way he was—when?—before high school, perhaps. But the moment those words filled the air, it was apparent to all of us that such a goal was not attainable and was not what anyone really wanted.

Later, after much talk, some anger, and some tears, a realistic goal appeared. They wanted Philip to be part of their family again, and they wanted him as part of their family life. They also wanted a better relationship with Jill.

The difficulty, of course, lay in Greg and Susie's unconscious fear of abandonment. On an unconscious level, they saw Philip as a kind of bonsai tree. They wanted to put copper wires on his arms and legs, forcing him back into his usual position in the family so that he could conform to the family norm.

Underlying everything they said was the implicit expectation—gathered by talking in the beauty parlor to our patient—that we had some magic way of fixing things. We were to make things right in Greg and Susie's family.

It was apparent to us that if there was to be peace in the family, there were going to have to be changes made—by Greg and

Susie and by Philip and Jill. We were going to have to find out if Greg and Susie were willing to do what had to be done to bring about change. Were they willing to manipulate their son and daughter-in-law in order to turn them around? Greg and Susie thought that sounded awful. They didn't like to think of themselves as manipulating anyone, let alone Philip.

"Maybe you better tell us what you've got in mind?" asked Greg.

"Well, if you're willing, we will teach you how to bring Philip—and Jill—back into the family."

They both nodded and stared at us, and we began an explanation of joining.

"When you have a family member who is doing something—and you want to persuade that family member to do exactly the opposite of what he is doing—you use a technique known as joining."[2]

"What's joining?" asked Susie.

"It works this way. Nobody likes to be told what to do. The more you put pressure on Philip to conform to your idea of how a youngest son should behave, the more he's going to rebel. But if you join his behavior, if you encourage him in his rebellion, he will give up that rebellion, turn around and do what you want."

Greg just stared at us.

"The only hitch is that you have to mean it when you join. If you say you're proud of the way he's made such a success of himself, you have to touch some part of yourself that believes that and put that belief in your voice. Otherwise he'll hear what you're saying as sarcasm and be angry."

As it usually does, it took a lot of convincing before Greg and Susie agreed to give joining a try. They talked about it between themselves, and the next time they saw Philip, Greg volunteered a statement.

"You know, Phil, I'm really proud of what you've done. Youngest V.P. in the company—that's really something!"

---

2. See chapter 1.

The experienced debater had trouble talking. There was moisture in his eyes. Then Philip just said "Thanks, Dad," but both Greg and Susie felt they had their son back at that moment. There was more to it than that, but they'd been so encouraged by Philip's initial response that it was easy to go on joining. And Jill got the same treatment. Praise of her housekeeping made her melt. When Susie actually talked to her, she found Jill thirsty for the attentions of an older woman, perhaps the mother she'd never had.

Somehow, without noticing what they were doing, Greg and Susie had accepted Philip's movement into management and the upward mobility of his life. But in so doing, they found he was coming home again, hanging around the house the way they'd always hoped he would.

An odd note about the bonsai tree: If you remove the copper wires that control it and force it into such strange and exotic and attractive shapes, the limbs, freed of their restraints, will slowly straighten and reach up to heaven. It becomes a different tree, less tortured, less fascinating, but in the eyes of some, more beautiful than ever.

Despite his seeming independence, Philip had been longing for approval from his father and mother; despite her poise and upper-class manners, Jill had been longing for a mother. Despite their feelings of hurt and abandonment, Greg and Susie had wanted their son back. It worked out.

David and Emily had a similar problem with their only child, their beloved son, Johnny, except that it was the opposite problem. David had been born into an affluent family that owned a chemical company. He was the third generation to head up the company, and a very nice company it was, too, highly profitable and with generous policies covering vacations and leisure time.

David ran the company with one hand, and with the other indulged his own passion for sailing and golf. Emily devoted herself with almost equal passion to a variety of charities. David and Emily knew they were among the luckiest people on the earth, to have been given so much. Not only had they been given much, but they enjoyed it.

The only blemish in their life was their inability to have more than one child. After Johnny, nothing. So he became the center of their world. His babyhood was a wonder. His toddler days were triumphant. He welcomed school and it welcomed him. Johnny was beautiful and outgoing, everybody's favorite. To David, he seemed a natural heir to the chemical company. David and Emily were proud parents indeed. They were enjoying their lives—and David's childhood—and looking forward to enjoying David as an adult.

It went wrong. They never really knew where. Sometimes they thought it was his second grade teacher who got him interested in spinning, weaving, and natural foods. Perhaps it was his high school science teacher who spoke so passionately about the environment. Johnny, in any case, became more and more interested in the world of nature as he went through school. His junior year of high school was devoted to SAVE OUR RIVERS. Naturally, David and Emily enjoyed his enthusiasms; they smiled knowingly, sure he would outgrow the "phase" he was in. Wrong again.

Johnny refused the chance to go to an Ivy League college, and he wouldn't even discuss majoring in chemistry, wherever he went. His final choice was the Colorado School of Mines where, as far as David and Emily could figure out, he majored in backpacking. He also acquired a girlfriend, Dorothy, from California, stunningly beautiful and as crazy as he was (David's and Emily's shared opinion at that time) about anything related to the environment. In fact, her ambition was to move to a cabin in the woods and become a potter, using local clays.

Johnny always came home at Easter and for Thanksgiving, but there was a great deal of tension in the house. Both David and Emily were suffering from unconscious feelings of being abandoned and both were acting out. David's acting out took the form of trying to offer unsolicited advice. David tried to talk to his son about "his future," and Johnny told his father he was one of the "older generation" and didn't understand about him and Dorothy. Emily's efforts took the form of criticizing Johnny for not showing enough "respect" to his father. Johnny told her he didn't think his father was showing enough respect for him. Bruised feelings resulted from those efforts at "communication." It was equally awkward to have Johnny and Dorothy at the country club, both in checkered shirts and boots. Despite looking out of place, Dorothy usually made a good impression on David's and Emily's friends because she was so beautiful—but it was clear that she and Johnny, through their dress, were making a statement. David was half out of his mind. Over and over, he tried to talk to Johnny but got nowhere. Emily just went into the bathroom, turned on the water, and wept.

The family then entered several years that could best be described as a time of misery for David and Emily. They watched— feeling confused and helpless as both Johnny and Dorothy got low-paying jobs with environmental organizations, and Dorothy began expanding on her hopes to become a potter. After three years of saving rivers, water, air, and the forests—while David stewed over who was going to take over the family chemical company—Johnny and Dorothy quit their jobs and moved to Vermont where they set up a small pottery business, everything hand-crafted, beautiful, and impractical. They lived without indoor plumbing and claimed to be thriving on it. Their shop (they called it their outlet) was barely more than a shack, but it was large enough to display their wares.

About the only times that David and Emily saw Johnny were at Easter and at Thanksgiving. Those occasions proved troublesome because Johnny and Dorothy were now living on a macrobiotic diet, although Emily had a sneaking suspicion that Johnny did still like her Thanksgiving table, which was traditional and ample.

Feeding them on those holidays wasn't fun because, while she served them her traditional meals rich in carbohydrates, sugar, and animal fats, she and David had to listen to enthusiastic lectures on the virtues of rice and beans and the bad, pernicious effect of sugar of almost any kind. Refined sugar seemed to be a demon of a special sort. David and Emily tried to be supportive of Johnny, but their hearts were never in it. Once or twice a year, David and Emily were invited up to Vermont where they were fed a variety of beans and struggled with being good sports about the backyard privy. Those occasions were strained, too.

It was immediately on return from an especially bad back-to-nature visit that Emily got in touch with us. She was experiencing a profound depression. It wasn't hard to determine why. Emily made the situation quite clear, but it wasn't until she invited David to come in for a joint session that we saw how deeply troubled this family was. Rich, privileged, and miserable.

Again, to simplify a great deal of talking and consideration of the situation, our recommendation was joining.

Later, David and Emily said it was the hardest thing they ever did. They began by throwing out most of the staples in their kitchen and restocking the house with all of the natural foodstuffs required to support a macrobiotic diet. They studied recipes and tried several dishes. They hated everything they made. But they persevered. On the phone to Johnny, they recounted their efforts and, having found one dish that they could at least swallow, they praised it to the sky. Johnny and Dorothy seemed pleased that Johnny's mother and father had joined them in their way of eating. Meanwhile, David and Emily began to go out to dinner. Every night. And to wait.

Sure enough, as it does every year, Thanksgiving rolled around, and as they always did, Johnny and Dorothy came down from Vermont for a family dinner. Now all of the effort that Emily and David had put into their new kitchen came to fruition. Instead of a beautifully browned Thanksgiving turkey, Emily served a white bean ragout. Instead of Johnny's two favorite dishes—candied yams topped with roasted marshmallows and jellied cranberry sauce—Emily served unsweetened sweet potatoes and homemade, unsweetened cranberry sauce, which they all had to admit was a little bit sour. Emily wondered aloud if she should have used honey, but reminded them all of Johnny's passionate declaration, "Honey is pure white sugar, that's all!" There was also a wild rice and brown rice casserole, stuffed mushrooms, onions in olive oil, and, instead of Emily's celebrated pumpkin pie, there was fresh fruit in molasses and fruit juice with a whole-wheat pie crust.

Sensing that Johnny's enthusiasm for Thanksgiving at home wasn't what it used to be, David and Emily found themselves really enjoying the meal. It was, David said later, the best Thanksgiving he ever had.

David and Emily plunged back into joining with a passion, animals in for the kill. The more they enthused about Johnny's and Dorothy's "sweet, charming, unspoiled" cottage and waxed eloquent over the "wonderful sense of well-being" they were getting from their macrobiotic diet, the more restless Johnny seemed to become. Patience, more patience, and a steady diet of joining led to change.

One evening that winter, Johnny called David and asked if he could come down and talk to him in his office. Johnny wouldn't say why he wanted to see his father but made it clear it was to be a business trip. On the appointed day, just in case Johnny came home to dinner, Emily made her white bean casserole.

Johnny expressed some frustration with his lifestyle. It was one thing to be potters—and the pottery that was being made under Dorothy's careful eye was indeed lovely—but Johnny could see that they were still living from hand to mouth, and he was tired of being poor. He asked his father to cosign a $150,000 loan so they could get larger quarters, hire some people, quadruple their output, and open a proper sales office in Manchester. David suggested that the family company could handle a $250,000 investment in

Johnny and Dorothy's enterprise, stating that he liked the product and would be glad to recommend it to the board.

Endless and painful joining had confirmed that "the apple doesn't fall very far from the tree," and a family reconciliation was in the works. It is true that David didn't persuade Johnny to take over the chemical company, but David's thinking is that running one company is like running another. He likes what he has been seeing of Johnny's management style (not very surprising, since it is quite similar to his own) and has the feeling that if he ever wants to give up the family company, Johnny might well be there.

Meanwhile, Johnny and Dorothy have shifted their main manufacturing plant one hundred miles to the south of Manchester, where they retain their main retail outlet, but are now one hundred miles closer to David and Emily, which means they will get to see their anticipated grandchild more often. Without a word of complaint from Johnny and Dorothy, David and Emily have given up their macrobiotic diet.

Now why do we call this our "Surprise Chapter"?

The reasons are simple. While it is true that joining is the principal technique that we were presenting to Greg and Susie and later to David and Emily, there were other goals being reached even though they were never discussed.

First of these was *giving up being critical*. For a long time, Philip (and later Philip and Jill) had experienced what seemed to be constant disapproval. Greg and Susie didn't like what was happening to Philip, and while they said very little, their disapproval was like a black cloud over family gatherings. Johnny and Dorothy had found themselves living under a similar cloud of criticism when they went to see David and Emily, who thoroughly disapproved of the choices they were making and didn't hesitate to say so. By inviting Greg and Susie to find something in Philip's life of which they could approve ("You know, Phil, I'm really proud of what you've done. Youngest V.P. in the company—that's really something!") and by persuading David and Emily to take up Johnny and Dorothy's macrobiotic diet, we had helped them shift focus from being negative to being positive. Instead of being disapproving, they were being approving. Philip and Jill were being accepted for the people they were. Johnny and Dorothy were being accepted for the people they were. If you want good relationships with your kids, a steady diet of acceptance will go a long way.

The second goal that was reached without ever being discussed was *giving up offering unsolicited advice*. The hidden messages in unsolicited advice are invariably of the "I-know-more-than-you-do" or of the "how-can-you-be-so-dumb" schools of child-raising, and whether you call those messages attacking or critical, you don't have to be a rocket scientist to see that they can really spoil family relationships.

Whether you look at it from a positive point of view ("a steady diet of acceptance will go a long way") or negative ("messages attacking or critical really spoil family relationships"), by being aware of the dangers of acting out when feeling abandoned, by accepting, by joining it is possible to bridge over the difficulties that arise when our kids go their own ways.

12

If Your Kid Commits a Crime

W hen we are talking about our kid having committed a criminal act, we are already on the wrong track because that phrase "our kid having committed a criminal act" suggests that our kid was responsible for the crime that was committed. Let us consider instead—and a most horrible recognition for us as parents—that a criminal act must be considered a family act, an expression of a family pathology that goes back to grandparents and probably to great-grandparents and beyond. If your kid commits a crime it is part of a family problem and must be dealt with—and treated—*as a family problem*, not as simply your kid's problem. The answer is for the family to go into treatment *immediately*.

You may consider getting treatment for the family after the criminal act has been committed as locking the barn door after the horse is gone. But that is not the case because the family illness that led to the act still exists, and unless it is treated, there will be more crimes, more acting out, possibly by other members of the family.

Where do you go? The answer is simple enough. Get in touch with your family doctor. If you don't happen to have a family doctor you can call any mental health professional and ask for guidance. Those of you who live in major cities where there are postgraduate schools that train mental health professionals may wish to look in the yellow pages for a psychological training institute that is convenient for you. An inquiry by telephone will tell you if the institute in your city has a *treatment service*. These treatment services provide low-cost psychological treatment—individual or family according to the orientation of the institute—that is professional, valuable, and affordable. Mental health professionals—including the people at these institutes—are people who are seeking to bring help to others. It's all right to phone them. Your call will be well received. You will not be imposing or intruding; quite the contrary.

Some of you may not be receiving the message of this chapter with understanding. You may feel that your kid did something terrible, and it is his or her fault and responsibility, and he or she should pay the price for what was done. What can be said here that would help you reexamine those beliefs? Would you consider a rather simple exercise that might be illuminating for you about the pathology in your own family? If you're willing, take a piece of paper and write down, as best you can, the family members—from your kid's generation, from your generation, from your parents' generation, and from your grandparents' generation—who suffered from emotional illness. Write down as well— again as best you can—the illnesses from which they suffered. Take some time. Of course you're not mental health professionals, and you may not be sure about Aunt Sophie or Grandfather Tim. Trust your own judgment. If Aunt Sophie was talking to the cows—and they were talking back—put her on the list; if Grandfather Tim was so depressed for the final fifteen years of his life that he seldom left the house, then put him on the list, too. Common sense will lead you to a reasonable assembly of your family members who've been troubled.

In making this list, we're talking here about psychotic illnesses (people who heard or saw or imagined things that weren't there), about depression (for which suicide is the ultimate symptom), and about alcoholism and various phobias, about people who went through life having periodic rages that had terribly negative effects on their lives, and about people whose lives were characterized by chronic episodes of trouble or difficulty. Other characteristics you might keep in mind are those of self-isolation, inability to hold a job, chronic, heated arguments or fights (known in our business as "interpersonal conflict"), and an inability to form either lasting friendships or lasting love relationships.

When you have made your list, you will see that your family, like every family in America, has its share of emotional illness. If your kid has committed a criminal act or an act of sexual abuse, we suspect you will find more emotional illness rather than less. You may also be able to detect the flow of illness from one generation to another.

How does pathology (mental illness) pass down from one generation to the next, usually getting worse generation by generation? The answer is simple enough. Let us suppose that when your grandmother was a baby she was raised in a troubled household in which she received very little nurturing. The end product of that would be that your grandmother, not having been nurtured when she was little, didn't know how to nurture your mother when she was little. Since mothers tend to do to their babies what was done to them when they were babies, the odds are high that your grandmother wasn't able to nurture your mother, and from that it follows that your mother probably wasn't able to nurture you. The same applies to fathers. Parents who were loved, nurtured, and respected rarely produce children of their own who commit criminal acts. So when your kid acts out by committing some socially forbidden act your kid is expressing the breakdowns in nurturing from many generations back.

In these situations, therapy, especially family therapy, can prove to be invaluable because it can break the pattern of pathology being passed on inexorably from generation to generation. In fact, an intervention (which is what professionals call therapy) may be the *only* way that you can stop that pattern from being repeated.

But we're concerned in this chapter with what you can do when you learn that your kid has committed a crime or an act of sexual abuse. The first thing, as we've said, is to get the whole family into treatment. The second thing goes hand-in-hand with the first: stand by your kid. Now you may find that hard to do. Your kid's action may offend you to the point that you feel like turning your back. Please don't; that will only make things worse. Condemn the crime if you need to, but do not condemn your kid. Rather, at the same time that you take steps to treat your kid's mental health, take steps to treat the realities of the situation. That usually means a lawyer. If money is a major issue the Legal Aid Society is often the place to turn to.

These are terrible situations. Our hearts go out to you.

13

If Your Kid Is Mentally Ill

W hen your kid is mentally ill, you and your family are affected in many unhappy ways. Perhaps the most pervasive problem that arises isn't always evident to us as parents at the onset of the illness. We're so preoccupied with the immediate problems at hand, that we don't recognize its potential longevity. Mental illness tends, in case after case, to go on and on and on. Recognizing that we, as parents, are often virtually obsessed with our kid's illness, it is equally important that we pay attention to ourselves and plan a way of dealing with the issues at hand, giving special attention to the long haul. In other words, the parents of mentally ill kids need support systems. Much of this chapter will deal with what you can do for yourselves.

Since most of you, at this moment, are almost unable to think about anything but the nagging worry that your kid is or might be mentally ill, let's begin with that. There are many painful subjects in this book, and the possibility of mental illness in our kids is among the most torturous. For some of us, the issue is no longer in doubt. Our kids were diagnosed in early childhood or during adolescence—as autistic, as a teenage schizophrenic, as suffering from attention-deficit disorder, or as mentally retarded—and we've lived with that knowledge ever since.

Look again at the word *suffering* in the previous sentence. It's really important to remember that when our kids are mentally ill, they're in pain. They're suffering. Keeping that in our consciousness will help us accept them and treat them with compassion. And recognize that you as parents are suffering as well and must also be treated with compassion. Being the parent of a mentally ill child is one of the special tortures of life.

While many mental illnesses are diagnosed when kids are little, many more of them are not detected until later. For too many parents, the realization that our kids might be mentally ill doesn't hit home until our kids are in their twenties. That's when the suspicion arises that there might be something wrong, and we begin watching our kid's behavior, trying to rationalize really disturbing conduct into some kind of normalcy, and, in spite of the unconscious denial to which so many of us fall victim, that's when we often tumble into the agony of allowing ourselves to fear the worst. It all adds up to days, weeks, months, even years of emotional anguish.

What do we do when our grown child is having unpredictable rages and sometimes seems filled with hate? How should we react to a kid who doesn't trust friends, who is convinced there are deadly forces nearby preparing to swoop down, who often feels attacked when others see no objective evidence of attack? How do we deal with our kid when he (yes, usually *he*, rarely *her*) suspects his spouse of infidelity? What do we say to him when we are painfully aware that what he is saying to us doesn't quite make any sense?

What should we do when our kid turns into a loner, usually finding a job in which there is little personal contact, having little or no social life, spending hours and hours alone in his or her room, and usually insisting, when questioned, that everything is "fine"?

How do we handle it when our kid begins to recount bizarre beliefs about being followed, poisoned, loved from a distance, or of being a person of inflated worth, power, or knowledge? We'd like to think that our kid is joking, but we're afraid that isn't the case. Part of the problem is that for a long time, we simply don't know what's wrong. We may see all sorts of troubling behavior and not know what we're looking at.

We're going to begin this chapter by examining some of the most common forms of serious mental illness, specifically schizophrenia, schizophrenia with paranoid features, paranoid personality disorder, bipolar disease (formerly known as manic depression), and major depression.

We're not going to discuss the psychotic ("crazy") delusions that sometimes accompany alcohol or substance abuse. Such behavior—known as drug induced psychoses—normally disappear when the substance is out of the system. While there may be psychotic episodes, the problems that you see are almost surely those of addiction rather than of mental illness.

It is important to remember that there is no one to blame when a mental illness appears. It is equally important to remember that the illnesses we're writing about are never the same in any two people. All of these illnesses may present themselves in small, medium, or large ways. Clearly the smaller versions are easier to understand and treat than the larger versions. Moreover, when mental illness appears, it does so not because we, as parents, have caused it, nor did our kids bring it on themselves.

We don't really know why people become mentally ill, but we do know a few things. The National Alliance for the Mentally Ill (NAMI) identifies seven especially significant facts about mental illness:

1. *There are genetic factors.* Mental illness tends to run in families. It is rare, when a patient has a specific illness, not to

find another family member (or members) with the same illness. So we know that some of our kids have a special
vulnerability to mental illness that isn't weak character but
rather the bad luck of being born into a family that has the
misfortune to be susceptible.

2. *We know there are biological factors.* There are biological
   brain diseases that interfere with normal brain chemistry.
3. *We know that life stresses may trigger the onset of symptoms*,
   which is a way of saying that a vulnerable kid in a low-stress,
   steady, life situation may not display symptoms of the disease, but let the life situation change for the worse—loss of
   a job, loss of a loved companion, bankruptcy, divorce—and
   the symptoms of the disease may appear.
4. *Mental illness is very common.* As many as 30.7 million
   Americans are affected in a single year. That's 16.7 percent
   of the population.
5. *Mental illnesses are equal opportunity diseases* affecting families regardless of age, race, income, religion, or education.
6. *Mental illness can be devastating for the whole family.* When
   a kid's thinking, feeling, and ability to relate to others are all
   disrupted, every family member is apt to be affected.
7. *There is treatment for mental illness.* Appropriate medical
   care and rehabilitation enable many people to recover, some
   fully and others enough to lead productive lives.[1]

With those general thoughts in place, let us take a look at some
of the more serious mental illnesses, after which we will glance
briefly at what are known as personality disorders. Let us begin
with schizophrenia, a mental illness that affects almost 1 percent
of the country, or about two million people. It may range in severity from minor strange behavior to a total catatonic state (frozen
in one physical position and emotionally unavailable). One pri-

---

1. From NAMI pamphlet "NAME Families Just Like Yours . . . "

mary characteristic of schizophrenia is the hearing of voices—although it is also characterized by your kid denying those voices. Many a mom or dad has felt a feeling of sinking horror upon noticing their kid staring off into space, obviously listening to something that no one else is hearing. Many a mom or dad has felt a feeling of terrible fear from knowing that if they'd ask the obvious question—"Honey, what're you listening to?"—all they would get in response would be a denial. "Nothing." Or "I'm not listening to anything."

Do you ever wonder what those voices say? They aren't very imaginative. One major theme is vilification. They attack your kid's self-esteem: "You're worthless! You're a piece of s—t! You should be dead!" Sometimes they try to take away all hope for the future: "You're so dumb! You'll never amount to anything! Give it up! You oughta be dead!" Sometimes they support other delusions: "Your boss is secretly in love with you." "This is the captain of the space ship *Zotec*, and I am talking to you from outer space." Sometimes the voices come in the from of coded messages from the radio. "This is your leader. Listen closely to my instructions."

Some schizophrenics see visual hallucinations: "Hey, how about that funny animal running up the wall?"

Schizophrenia may also produce incoherent or disorganized speech. Your kid rambles and just doesn't quite make sense. There may be withdrawal and a curious flatness of speech, words seemingly without feelings. Sometimes there is grossly disorganized behavior—the ability to work and personal hygiene deteriorate. But schizophrenia is primarily identified by delusions and/or hallucinations.

One curious item about schizophrenia: If the disease comes on quickly and reaches a fullblown, or florid state, quite rapidly, it is likely to be more responsive to treatment than schizophrenia that comes on slowly over many months or years.

Schizophrenia with paranoid features—often referred to as

paranoid schizophrenia—is also characterized by delusions and voices. But these delusions usually involve feelings of persecution—"the FBI is tapping my phone," "my neighbors are watching me." The voices frequently reinforce those delusions—"your neighbor wants to kill you." Paranoid schizophrenics are full of hate, tend to see conspiracies all around them, and are frequently loners because there is no one out there they can trust. These are people who join hate groups and cults. These are the people who sometimes commit acts of violence—in self-defense according to the bizarre thinking that characterizes their illness.

In contrast to paranoid schizophrenia, there is a paranoid personality disorder, which may occasionally display brief psychotic episodes but for the most part does not include the psychotic delusions or hallucinations of the paranoid schizophrenic. Rather, the child (usually male) is coldly rational and, in his own way, logical. He is characterized by excessive suspiciousness, hostility, and hypervigilance. The paranoid personality blames others, instantly attacks perceived insults, and may frequently become involved in lawsuits. Moments of grandiosity—a preposterously inflated sense of self—are common. Since one of the characteristics of the paranoid personality disorder is that he does not think there is anything wrong with him—it is others who are in the wrong—it is difficult, if not impossible, to get these kids to go for help.

Bipolar disorder (formerly referred to as manic depression) refers to a disease that alternates between two extreme moods: a manic mood—sometimes called mania (feelings of great excitement)—and a depressed mood (the "blues"). The manic state really needs no description. There is an extraordinary sense of well-being, a high. Your kid's feet will seem not to be touching the ground; he or she will be so grandiose, talking so rapidly, ideas racing, planning, playing, existing on three hours of sleep, and will be so busy phoning, buying, selling, that you will know you're looking at a manic episode. It is terrifying and you can't miss it. There is a lesser form of this illness called hypomania, in which the high isn't quite as exaggerated, but when the excited, flamboyant behavior goes on for three or four days, you should know what you are seeing.

The manic mood, which has been known to occur every few months, often alternates with a depressive mood in which your kid will be as sad as he or she was previously glad. There will be a profound loss of interest in life or in pleasure of any kind. There may be weight loss, a lack of energy, insomnia, or too much sleep. Nothing you can do or say will get your kid going. Pointing out reality ("It's a beautiful day outside") doesn't help.

Bipolar disease sometimes fails to present the manic mood. All that is seen is the depressive mood—in which instance the illness is called unipolar disease. A bipolar or unipolar depression can be a very severe depression indeed.

There is also another, different kind of depression that is called major depression, and it is impossible to tell by looking whether you're dealing with a bipolar or unipolar depression or a major depressive episode. In all cases, they're treated as depression. The only way to tell them apart is by which medication works, usually lithium in the case of bipolar or unipolar depression or an antidepressant in the case of major depression. In both cases some form of antidepressive medication is almost certainly called for.

We must mention another category of mental illness known as personality disorders. These afflict many of our kids, and they are disheartening conditions since they share one very troubling characteristic. Your kid doesn't believe there's anything wrong and won't accept the suggestion that it would be a good idea to get some help. The personality disorders are:

paranoid personality disorder
schizoid personality disorder
schizotypal personality disorder
antisocial personality disorder

borderline personality disorder
histrionic personality disorder
narcissistic personality disorder
avoidant personality disorder
dependent personality disorder
obsessive-compulsive personality disorder[2]

The previous edition of the DSM used to list alcoholic personality disorder, and, while it is not included in the current listing, many of you will recognize in the alcoholics of your acquaintance an almost universal denial that they are alcoholic or that anything is wrong and a refusal to get help.

All of these conditions range from mild to severe, and all of them can cause your kid grief in his or her ability to negotiate the difficulties that are part of life, primarily difficulties in family relationships, personal relationships, and the area of work. These are conditions that endure over time. Unless treated, they are almost certain to last for a lifetime These conditions are very hard to treat primarily because it is almost impossible to get these kids into treatment. The paranoid personality disorder, about which we wrote a little earlier in this chapter, is a case in point. The fault is always with others—the kid has done nothing wrong; there is a rational structure built around the idea that someone is out to get him, to hurt him, to kill him, and *that's* the problem. There's nothing wrong with him, and he isn't going to go to any head-shrinker whom he will probably suspect is part of the conspiracy against him.

Whether the difficulty is paranoid thinking, antisocial behavior, self-isolating behavior, or any of the other personality disorders, the hope for the future is not great.

However, that gloomy assessment does not apply to the major

---

2. As identified in the *Diagnostic and Statistical Manual of Mental Disorders* (DSM-IV), American Psychiatric Association, Washington, D.C., 1994, 629ff.

mental illnesses that we discussed earlier in the chapter. It is important for us as parents to remember that there are treatments for the major illnesses we've just been looking at. A combination of psychological support—often talking to someone—and medication do offer hope. Sometimes treatment works brilliantly and brings about a cure. Other times it is less successful but at least puts the patient into a holding pattern that enables some degree of functioning and provides a relatively "normal" life. It is difficult to generalize about mental illness. Each situation depends on the individual illness and the individual patient.

What do you do when you find yourself looking at disturbing symptoms? Begin by saying nothing to your kid.

Instead, as in so many other troublesome situations, it is recommended that you begin by setting out on a journey to find out more about what you're facing. One good way to start is by consulting the health professional easiest for you to reach. That may mean your personal physician, a nurse who lives nearby, or a local mental health clinic. Find someone you trust, feel you can talk to, and tell that person what you've been seeing—*in detail*. Small anecdotes about your kid can provide a great deal of information to a health professional.

There are many specialists in the mental health community. They include psychiatrists (medical doctors who specialize in emotional disorders and who are your principal source of medication, as only a doctor can write a prescription), psychologists (specialists who are *not* doctors but who have earned a doctorate in psychology and who are often specially trained in testing, evaluation, and the clinical treatment of the mentally ill), and social workers (who have much hands-on experience with patients and who are familiar with the entire medical system and what it can make available).

A word here on behalf of social workers. Some people look down on them as hopelessly idealistic "do-gooders," but if you have a mentally ill child, you might want to kiss the ground your social worker walks on. In many situations, social workers will not only give you information that you need but will also direct you to other sources of help. Beyond that, most mental health professionals are overworked and have severe limits on their time. Social workers—who share the problem of excessive case loads and limited time—may still be the people most likely to be able to sit with you, talk with you, and answer your questions. Many times, when we're in a mental health facility, we're so anxious we can't even remember all the questions we wanted to ask. Social workers will often be patient until your anxiety diminishes and you can ask the questions you need to ask.

Please pay special attention to your own emotional health. The anxiety, distress, and grief you experience over a mentally ill child, if untreated, can impair your ability to help. These are profoundly difficult situations; you need to have all your resources available and working. Even in that initial consultation, don't limit yourself to what your kid needs; ask where you can get some support for yourself. When you take care of yourself, you take care of your kid.

Usually, after you have consulted one or two or three professionals—none of whom will have seen your kid—you will have, at least, an educated guess as to the nature of the problem. Hopefully, you will also have an idea of some sort of a support system for yourself—a social worker to whom you can talk, a group that will provide information and support.

After you have done your homework is the time you may want to speak to your kid. You may very well think it would be wise to take your kid to a mental health facility for evaluation. You may have found a hospital with a good mental health program; you may have found a local mental health clinic. Talk to your kid about what you have learned. One way of starting that most difficult conversation is to say that you've observed that your kid seems to be in some sort of emotional pain, and you'd like to help him or her get some relief.

The important thing for your kid at this moment is to *not* feel abandoned. You might propose—and here you might ask your kid for permission—that you phone for an appointment for you both. You, or course, will go in to the appointment with your kid. Sometimes one parent goes in, sometimes both. Do whatever is going to make it easier for your kid.

Assuming that your kid agrees to a consultation what will happen?

Your kid should get a complete workup, beginning with a physical examination to determine if there might be any physical reason for his symptoms. If that happens to be the case, you may find yourself dealing with a physical problem rather than with mental illness. Such things do happen but not very often. Far more likely, there will be no physical cause for your kid's behavior, and attention will focus on his mental state. An examination will be made of your kid's mental status and a tentative or working diagnosis may be made. Sometimes your kid may be asked to remain in a hospital while his evaluation is being completed; other times, your kid will be given some medication and sent home with you.

At this point, you have to prepare yourself for a long period of anxiety. Finding the right treatment for your kid, the right medication, and the right dosage, can be a long and frustrating experience. As each one of us is unique, so your kid is unique. Drugs that work on a hundred people may not work on the hundred and first. If too small a dose is given, the drug may have no effect. If too large a dose is given, there may be side effects your kid can't live with. Having the stamina and the patience to test one, two, three, four drugs is no easy matter. It puts a strain on any household.

However, you have begun a course of treatment for your kid. You've obtained the best medical advice available to you, and a process is underway. By this time, you are far more knowledgeable about your kid's illness—if that's what it is—and you're learning the medical system. So you're far ahead of where you were a few days or weeks or months earlier.

Let's pause for a moment to ask a horrible question. What if your kid refuses to go in for that consultation? What if your kid insists that such an evaluation is unnecessary? Take a deep breath and remember that it is not your kid who is causing you pain. It is the illness. And if your kid won't go with you to a mental health professional, you can't even be sure which illness you're dealing with.

All of your impulses will be to argue and to apply pressure. You know that speaking to a professional is the right thing to do. And you're right. But arguing, pressuring, threatening, attempting to persuade or force your kid to go in for a consultation is, unhappily, almost always the wrong thing to do. Unless your kid's situation has reached the point where you're prepared to call the police and ask them to take your kid into the hospital for an involuntary confinement, it is most unlikely you'll be able to be persuasive. Most parents do not want to call the cops to come for their child and will only do so if the situation is far out of control. If you do call the police, you will have to add your kid's resentment to the list of problems with which you're struggling.

It's very tough to accept your kid's decision, but it is usually the only thing you can do. Tell him or her that you understand that decision, that you have some idea of how frightening going in for a consultation could be. Say that you have an idea that your kid is in pain. You have some idea of how painful it can be to be frightened and confused, and you understand not wanting to do anything. Try to get across the idea that all you want is to suggest that there is help available, if your kid wants help.

Can children who are mentally ill really be treated? Can treatment cure them? If they are cured, can the cure be permanent? Can a cure be only temporary? Can there be complete recovery? Is there a possibility your kid could be stronger after treatment than before the sickness set in? Is there a possibility your kid will always be fragile? The answer to all those questions is yes.

The difficulty in trying to assess the prospects for your kid is that each case is individual. Consider some of the following vignettes:

> Janet was a sweet, bright, outgoing, only child of an ultrarich family in Dallas when voices began to tell her to take off all her clothes and run through the streets. She did so and soon wound up surrounded by police. When they approached her, she turned savage, and it took three officers to subdue her, one of whom was badly bitten in the face. Janet was then hospitalized, where she cowered in her bed, terrified of everyone and snarling. One of the newer antipsychotic medications, Risperdal, was prescribed. The effect it had was truly miraculous. Janet was transformed back into the sweet, bright, outgoing child she had always been. Unfortunately, that was not the end of the story. If Janet had remained on Risperdal, a drug reportedly free of the harsh side effects of earlier antipsychotics, she could have been sustained indefinitely, possibly being helped in her recovery by a course of talking therapy. But Janet complained about the way Risperdal made her feel. It robbed her of any highs. She felt "blah," and she refused to take it. Nothing her devoted father and mother could say to her was persuasive. When she went off the medicine, the illness returned. Janet lives now in a squalid shanty town on the edge of Tijuana in the company of drifters and others who are mentally ill. Her housing is always temporary, always filthy, as is she. And there is nothing her family can do. She refuses to listen.

> Antony was the son of highly educated New England parents. He was well-bred, well-spoken, had just graduated from college, and was preparing to move to New York City to pursue a career in publishing when he mentioned to his family that, in addition to looking for work, he would also be doing some preaching. They were surprised. In response to their question, he explained that he was Jesus Christ and had many responsibilities to the poor. Again, the onset of the illness had been quick, and antipsychotic medication produced very satisfactory results. Antony became his old self again, and he was able to

tolerate the medication. More than that, he realized that he was sick and modified his plans. Instead of moving to New York City, which he knew would be a high-pressure situation, he found a teaching job in a Maine small town and went into a talking therapy. After a few years of cementing his recovery, he married and fathered four children. While Antony is considered by some to be a little odd he has survived his break, gone off the medication, finished his therapy, and lives a rewarding life.

Joey, last of eleven children in a large blue-collar family, had an early childhood marked by tantrums. He never seemed to get enough. When he wasn't asking for more than his share, he was argumentative and aggressive. At the age of fourteen, he tried to hang himself, and that resulted in his first hospitalization. He spent the next ten years in and out of mental hospitals, tormented by the conspiracies he knew were operating against him. The FBI was tapping his phone; the neighbors wanted to kill him; his teachers were conspiring together to keep him from graduating. By the time he was twenty-six, his agoraphobia—fear of open spaces—and his paranoid thinking had taken control of him. It was impossible for him to leave his family's home alone.

His parents—who had been desperate about him for years—finally had a bit of luck. They met a social worker who came to the house and persuaded Joey to go with her to see a psychiatrist she knew. This was another triumph for antipsychotic medication. The feelings of being persecuted and of being a victim of conspiracies left him. He was still sometimes aware of such thoughts, but he knew they were part of his illness and ignored them. Joey went into therapy, both individual and group, and is slowly moving toward a normal life.

These brief vignettes are intended to show you that there is no predictable course for mental illness. Rather, each case is individual. All you can do is the best you can for your kid—and for yourself. Let us look further at how you can get help.

At this point (when you have faced the difficulty of acknowl-edging mental illness and taken the first steps to get your kid into treatment, or at least have attempted to do so), it is vital that you do something for yourself. The stress a parent undergoes with a mentally ill child is enormous. Many parents—who like to think of themselves as stoic and tough—have broken down under the ongoing strain of caring for a mentally ill child. One difficulty is that many parents feel ashamed or stigmatized because they have a mentally ill kid. It is our hope that if you are having such feel-ings you can overcome them. Unless you can push them aside, they will only cause damage to you and to your kid. There *is* help available, and it is our recommendation that you shop among the many places where you can get support and select what you feel will be most beneficial to you in your particular situation.

One of the things that startles parents who are new to the world of the mentally ill is the quantity and variety of support that is available. There are the medical facilities—hospitals and clinics and other sources of treatment and there are numerous profes-sional and voluntary groups who will welcome you. NAMI —The National Alliance for the Mentally Ill, headquartered in Washington, D.C., acts as a support group for the local D.C. community and as a clearinghouse for local support groups all over the United States. A phone call to the NAMI Helpline in Washington, D.C. (1-800-950-NAMI) will enable you to get the names and phone numbers of the facilities and groups that assist the mentally ill in your community.

When you reach your local group—my wife and I, practicing in New York City, are familiar with AMI—The Alliance for the Mentally Ill, and with FAMI—Friends and Advocates of the Mentally Ill—both reachable at 212-684-FAMI. You will find them sensitive and generous with their time. They are New York affiliates of NAMI, have great expertise in the problems of the mentally ill, and, like other support groups all over the country, can be enormously helpful. Beyond that there are the self-help groups that provide an abundance of help. Many of these self-help groups offer some of the same benefits of the Buddy System (see chapter 9).

Parents of a newly diagnosed schizophrenic, usually frightened, confused, and sometimes overloaded with information about a disease they wish they'd never heard of, can find great comfort and reassurance in meeting with other parents of schizophrenics, people who have been there. At this writing, there are thirty-two different support groups in the greater New York area. And wherever you are, in the far west, the midwest, the south, or New England, you will find NAMI affiliates and numerous volunteer support groups.

Mental illness is a great tragedy, but we can make it better or worse, depending on how we react. If we do our homework, reach out to get help for our kid and for ourselves, and allow the miracles of modern medicine to provide help, we can comfort ourselves with the knowledge that we have done everything we could for our afflicted child.

14

If Your Kid Divorces

When we as parents are faced with the prospect of our kid's divorce—and we're concerned about the people involved—about our kid, perhaps about the person who is soon to become our kid's "ex," and very possibly about our grandchildren, as well as about other families we have come to know since the original marriage—it is a good idea to bear in mind the celebrated passage from the very wise Greek physician of the fourth century B.C., "First, do no harm."

Divorce can be a terrible trap for us as parents. It can be one of the most excruciating emotional experiences we'll ever go through. Certainly, divorce is high on the list of life's catalog of personal tragedies—the death of a child, the death of a loved one, bankruptcy, and being fired—not necessarily in that order—are considered life's most traumatic personal experiences because they involve disappointments and losses for so many people.

As parents, we have to watch the divorcing couple lose so many hopes and dreams, and sometimes material things as well, while their children (if there are children), are caught in the middle of a marital war and often pay a dreadful, often lifelong, emotional price in low self-esteem ("If I'd been good, Daddy wouldn't have left us . . .") and in an inability to trust ("If Mommy can leave, then anyone can leave me . . .").

Again, let us remind you of the dictum that appears so often in this book. In many seemingly critical situations, it is often best to do nothing, at least until you know the general situation better. When a divorce is announced, we certainly recommend that at the beginning it is often best not to take sides but simply to express regret at the whole situation. An expression such as "Oh dear, I'm sorry" might very well be the most appropriate response. An expression such as the one that follows is *not* recommended. We know one kid who announced a divorce and her mother, Daphne, chimed in with an enthusiastic, "Good riddance! The whole family has always hated the little son-of-a-bitch!"

Do we have to tell you there was a reconciliation? Do we have to tell you that the relationship between Daphne and her daughter was irreconcilably damaged by that one impulsive remark? And will you allow us to tell you that one primary reason that divorce is a trap for parents is that it creates so many opportunities for us to make that kind of mistake? Too often, when we witness the breakup of our kid's marriage, we swing from tragic dismay at one extreme to righteous satisfaction at the other, and too often we find ourselves blurting out sentiments that we later regret.

As you know by this time, one of the major themes of this book is that blaming and/or criticism, is almost invariably counterproductive. This is especially true when there is a divorce, and we have so many impulses to blame our kid or to come down firmly on the side of our kid, both of which are probably wrong. If at all humanly possible, neither partner should be abandoned.

Of course, the analytic preference in such a situation is to keep on talking and trying to understand and to wait before taking any action, especially before taking any action that involves siding with one of the partners against the other. Loving support, with expressions of sadness if that is what you are feeling, should be the order of the day.

One of the things that helps us as parents to navigate the difficult emotional waters of a divorce is to be very clear about our own personal goals. Curiously that is not as easy as it sounds. We would like to think that each of us knows what we want, but it is our experiences as therapists that people frequently are out of touch with their feelings and often don't know what they want. When parents are cut off from their real feelings, they often act on an emotional impulse ("Good riddance! The whole family has always hated the little son-of-a-bitch!"), assuming that if it feels right at the moment it must represent a personal goal.

Consider the mother who made that particular tactless and hurtful remark. When Daphne said it, she was convinced she wanted her son-in-law out of her life. But did she really? He was, after all, the father of her grandchildren, and despite his shortcomings as a husband, he had always been a good and dedicated father; and despite his shortcomings as a husband, he was still her daughter's principal source of financial support for her children and for herself in the future. Beyond that, she had to know somewhere that there was always the possibility of a reconciliation.

When Daphne thought about it later, she realized that she was enraged at the way her daughter had been treated (there was another woman—who, as it turned out, didn't last), and Daphne was still nursing numerous complaints about the way her son-in-law had spoken to her. (She was often offended by his tone of voice.) She spoke impulsively because she was so angry at her son-in-law that she lost touch with her own personal goals. She couldn't keep herself from popping off, which, after the reconciliation, proved very much to her disadvantage.

What would have served her better?

To begin, loving support for her kid would have been swell. She could have encouraged her kid to talk and listened empathetically without offering advice—unless it was requested—and then volunteered to provide any help she could. What did her daughter need from her that she could do?

Notice that in so doing she would be controlling the desire to speak or act impulsively or to give any of the dreaded unsolicited advice. She would also be avoiding the impulse to take refuge in rationality, which is another way of staying out of touch with feelings. Many of us as parents think that by being logical we are acting in a way that will help us reach our goals, but in being rational, many of us are cutting ourselves off from the feeling parts of ourselves. Instead of taking the time for inner exploration to find out what it is we really want, we fall back on what seems reasonable, what seems rational, what should be our goals—and we remain cut off from our real selves.

It is our recommendation that parents, caught in these painful situations, avoid acting either on emotional impulse or on emotionless rationality. Rather, we recommend that parents take the time to seek out their own feelings and goals and consider them. Then take time to consider an action. That's easy to say, but some of us have difficulty seeking out our own feelings and goals. How do we discover personal goals that may be buried deep within us under years of intellectualizing? We can offer you one approach.

Why not begin with a quiet, calm place and a piece of time when the passions of the moment or of the day are subdued. A cold drink in hot weather or a hot drink in cold weather is sometimes helpful. Then, when you have a situation in which your emotions are at least somewhat under control, it is wonderful to have a buddy to talk to (see chapter 8). If you don't have a buddy, pick someone as close as possible to fulfilling that role, who will allow you to talk without rushing in with solutions—possibly even your husband or your wife.

In this particular exercise, it is important to minimize talking about your kid and the details of the divorce. Concentrate instead on yourself. Talk quietly together about what the divorce means to *you*. Not to your kid, not to your grandkids, but to *you*. Give yourself permission to have all your feelings. You may be experiencing intense feelings of failure as a parent; you may be terribly humiliated that your kid's marriage has failed and all the neighbors will know; you may be reexperiencing some of the pain you went through when your own parents' marriage broke up. Whatever you have stored away inside you should be put into words and considered. Do you want to punish your about-to-be-ex-son-in-law because he reminds you of the way your father treated your mother? If that's the case, then you want to talk about that situation until you really have it clear that your son-in-law is *not* your father, and you shouldn't use old anger to punish him. That's the kind of thing we all wrestle with.

Some parents fear that having their feelings will be an overwhelming experience that will force them to act impulsively. Not so. It won't happen if you sit quietly and have your feelings—study them, weigh them, and consider what would be in your own best interest, in the best interest of your kid, your grandkids, and the ex who is about to be. If you are able to cry, if you are able to rage, you will find that you have passed through a doorway of healing.

One of the goals you might recognize in yourself is that you want your kid to be protected, in every way. Is your kid in any danger from the about-to-be-ex? If there is a history of battering—or even a suspicion—then it's time to be very careful and to take whatever precautions seem appropriate. You may want to consult an attorney (or the Legal Aid Society) to get an idea of the appropriate laws in your state and how they might apply to your kid's situation. Notice that all of these steps could be categorized under the heading of "getting information." Only when you know as much as possible about your kid's situation, your kid's wishes, and your own goals can you begin to formulate what to do, if anything.

Let us tell you a sad story about Solomon, a forceful man who took his self-appointed position as head of a large family very seriously. When his daughter Annie put her husband David out of the house and announced that she was getting a divorce, Solomon rushed in with accusations and succeeded not only in making a bad situation worse but really in destroying the life possibilities of his grandchild.

Solomon announced that he was opposing the divorce. He wouldn't listen to Annie's complaints about David, who happened to be one of Solomon's valuable employees. He refused to help Annie financially since all she had to do to solve her financial difficulties, according to his judgmental thinking, was to take David back. Solomon refused to help Annie with money for his grandchild, Zack. Instead, he turned his back on the entire situation. It was "her problem," and it was up to her to work it out. David continued to work for Solomon and refused to pay Annie any support money. She went to court, but the law moves very slowly in cases involving conflict, and she was soon out of money.

Annie, who was as pigheaded as her father, refused to be forced to stay in a marriage that was making her miserable. Instead, she left her child with her neighbor (who, it was learned years later, abused him physically and sexually) and got a full-time job. It was ten years before Solomon relented, and by that time, his grandchild had been classified as learning disabled and was displaying symptoms of the abuse to which he had been subjected. His only grandchild grew up to be an insecure, frightened, self-isolating man incapable of keeping a job. It was a tragedy for himself, for his mother, and for his grandfather.

Unfortunately, bad things do happen in life, and divorce can be one of them. For us as parents it is often traumatic. We may be faced with emotional demands for which we are not prepared; we may be faced with financial demands for which we are not prepared. But if we respond lovingly—and realistically—it can bring new closeness to our kid (and possibly our grandkids) and into our lives, and we may find that there are rewards in unhappy situations.

15

A Care Package for Parents: When Your Grandkids Are Your Concern

It has occurred to us that you might like some tips on how your kids can raise their kids so that your grandchildren grow up to be emotionally healthy and are psychologically conditioned to lead loving, productive lives. The following, while not a guarantee, will go a long way in that direction. Tell your kids we recommend that they:

DON'T BLAME, DON'T CRITICIZE

If your kids want to produce children who are timid, have difficulty making decisions, and generally suffer from what is known as low self-esteem, a steady diet of blaming and criticism will do the trick. The voice of a parent is the voice of a hundred. Consider those phrases that are too much a part of too many a childhood:

"You're a bad boy!" (or girl)
"What a dummy you are!"
"Don't you ever think of anyone except yourself?!"

Children believe what their parents tell them. Children who hear those phrases will grow up having been told by the greatest authority figures they will ever know that they are bad and stupid. One of the great lessons we have learned about raising children is that you deal with the action rather than with the child's character. You never criticize the child; you do, on occasion, criticize what the child did. It's all in the way you say it. The feelings underlying the words have to be love for your child and anger about your child's behavior.

"Hitting your sister hurts her and might make her sad!"
"Sisters are not for hitting!"
"Leaving the bathtub running and going out of the room is not a good idea!"
"Bathtubs are not for leaving!"
"You need to do a better job at sharing!"
"Your brother might feel angry and hurt when you take his toy!"

These reprimands do not attack a child's fundamental view of himself or herself.

DON'T OFFER UNSOLICITED ADVICE, (WHICH INCLUDES NOT PROVIDING HELP UNLESS IT IS REQUESTED)

If you rush in with advice before your child asks for it, the message you are sending is that your child couldn't handle the situation —wasn't smart enough, wasn't able to work hard enough, wasn't good enough. Parents who dedicate themselves to overseeing their children's homework, usually in the name of getting good grades and essentially doing the homework themselves, are teaching their children that they can't do it themselves, and that the other kids are smarter. What a terrible lesson!

If you want to build self-confidence, support your children with positive reinforcement.

"That's very good! I think it might be even better if you do it one more time!"

WHENEVER POSSIBLE—FROM THE EARLIEST DAY OF INFANCY—ALLOW YOUR KID TO CONTROL THE RUDDER OF HIS OR HER BOAT

Give them as many choices as you can. When it doesn't matter to you, let the kid choose. In response to "What should I wear?" try "Put on anything you like. You have good taste." If it does matter and you want your kid to look a certain way, lay out two or three shirts that are acceptable to you and ask "Which one would you like to wear?"

Some of these ideas are taken from a wonderful book called *Between Parent and Child* by Dr. Hyman Ginott. We've never forgotten how right it seemed when we read his suggestion that when our kid asked "Can I go out?" Instead of answering "Yes" or "No"—and reminding him that he is little and we are big—we could answer "If you want to" thereby giving him a sense of choice and power. Those little things are so little and yet so wonderful for your kid.

TEACH YOUR KID TO LOVE YOU WHEN HE OR SHE GROWS UP

Did you know that can be done? It's the simplest thing in the world. When your kid grows up, he or she will treat you the way your child was treated in infancy and early childhood. If you are sweet and loving when your child was little, then you will be treated with sweetness and love when he or she is grown.

16

When They Tell You that You've Been A Rotten, No-Good Parent and You're Afraid They're Right

No matter how hard we try, there comes a time when they tell us what's wrong with us. When they were teenagers, it hurt, but we thought we understood it because we figured it was part of their growing up. "Teenagers are like that," we said to ourselves. But when our twenty-four-year-old or our thirty-four-year-old tells us about the bad things we did and the good things we failed to do—and we have a sneaky feeling or a recognition that the things that are being said might very well be true—what do we do?

If we've read this book and we've absorbed that attitude toward children that it proposes then the answer is clear, in spite of the feelings that are aroused in us—guilt, anger, whatever—we have to keep our mouths shut and *listen*.

This is a critical moment in our relationship with our grown children. They have opened a door and given us a chance to repair the things that went wrong when we were raising them. And the way we repair those wrongs is to admit that there is truth in what they are saying. We know our kid is pouring out his or her own emotional truth. And then we apologize. We can even explain why we failed them—provided we do so briefly—and tell them how sorry we are that we didn't do better.

But that's it. We are not to be turned into whipping posts. We are not there to be a wailing wall for our kids to moan at. That's not good for them. After we have heard what they have to say and have agreed or disagreed and made the amends, we honestly feel are necessary, that's it! It is not healthy for them to go from an honest getting-it-off-their-chest, meaningful expression of feeling about the deficits in their childhoods to using Mom and Dad as figures to be abused. That is definitely not permissible.

Remember Sally and her daughters, Jane (the one who required dialysis) and Nancy? Well, after Sally had succeeded in dealing with Jane's problems, she began to catch a lot of flak from Nancy. She had to deal with Nancy's angry perception that she was her mother's second-favorite daughter and not her first. Sally listened to diatribes from Nancy about this for a long time. Finally, she said, "Okay, Nancy, this is it. You have one more time to get your resentments of me off your chest. Go for it. 'Cause this is your last chance."

Nancy started to talk about her father. "No," Sally said. "This is to be about you and me. Take your quarrels with your dad to him." Well, Nancy got down to it. Some of it was from long ago— from the time Jane got the Barbie doll, and she got the Alexandra doll that nobody could possibly want—to Sally's less-than-perfect response to Nancy's announcement that she was gay.

Sally didn't say anything. She just listened as her therapist had suggested.

Finally Nancy screamed, "See, you just sit there. Haven't you heard anything I've said?"

That was enough. "Stop yelling and sit down," Sally said. Nancy threw herself on the couch. "Nancy, what do you want from me now?"

"I want you to love me best," Nancy sobbed.

Sally waited for the sobbing to subside and then sat down by Nancy. "You should always be loved best," she said.

Nancy looked at her as if not hearing right. Then she burst out laughing. "Gee, what a little kid I am."

Sally put her arms around her and asked, "Would you like me to tell you how I love you? What I admire about you? What is special about you for me that no one else but you is? There are individual qualities and quirks about all my children that are embedded in my heart. It may have seemed to you I loved your sister more because she's always had that kidney problem, and I had to worry about her more. It isn't a question of a measurement of love. My love for each of you is made up of what so distinctly makes up each one of you. Can I tell you this? None of you children is interchangeable. None of you is replaceable. Shall I tell you about the unique love I have just for you? It must be so awful to feel second best."

Sally didn't wait for an answer but started a litany of all the special events, moments, and qualities that made Nancy special for her.

That was an easy one. Some resentments kids have toward their parents may be more toxic. There may be good reasons for this. At any rate, if our kid can't let those resentments toward us go and has to keep harping on them, we have to take a page from the life of John Feeny.[1]

John had been going through active alcoholism when his kids were small and had caused no end of grief to his wife and kids. Eventually he recovered, made amends to all, turned into a good family man, and was able to be a caring father. But his oldest son couldn't let the past go. Finally, John had to say, "I realize you had a terrible time as a kid due to my drinking. We've talked about it many times. You know that I am sorry, but there's nothing more I can do about it. If you need to vent your anger and sadness

---

1. One of Paul's patients, an actor who spent much of his life drinking and later straightened out to become a fine husband and father.

about me you will have to go to a therapist, or to Al-Anon, or to your friends. It won't do any good for us to keep at this hammer and tongs. This is the last I am going to hear from you about my drinking days."

John Feeny later had a slip and was on the edge of going back to the kind of drinking that had destroyed so many years. Luckily, he got back to his program and with the support of AA, friends, a psychiatrist who gave him an antidepressant, and a CSW who helped him sort out what got him off the wagon, he regained his sobriety.

His son loved it and used the slip to start berating his father. Feeny rightfully allowed not a word of it. "My disease is not your business. I will not discuss it with you. Get help with your own issues and leave me to mine." John's kid had the controlling personality of many kids of alcoholic parents. To make a long story short, John's kid got his help. John got his. Healthy boundaries between parent and kid were set up. Instead of a kid and his father solving Dad's problems, two adults started individually to solve their own individual problems.

Consider instead the story of Louise. This remarkable woman was one of the worst parents we have ever heard of outside of tabloid headlines until her children were in their late teens. If Louise could do anything for them after the childhood she gave them, any parent can fix up their mistakes. With Herculean courage and hard work, she went a long way to making things right. She, like Hercules, had a veritable Augean stable of mess to clean out before that was possible. Her story teaches us that the only way we can mitigate the damage we may have caused our kids is to achieve recovery from the shortcomings that made us unable to nurture them healthily in the first place. Then we can let them know that we understand how hurt they have been by us, but now the future is here and things can get better. Finally, by making amends to them in both words and deeds, we can help them learn for themselves that there are miracles of healing available for both them and us.

It was my privilege to work with and treat this magnificent woman who taught me as much as I taught her. If her story doesn't inspire us, we aren't capable of getting inspiration.

Louise came from a very poor Puerto Rican family. Her parents had come to New York hoping for a better life but didn't find it. Her father died when she was five. Her mother sometimes had to beg to get food for herself and Louise. Sometimes her mother was able to get jobs cleaning houses. She would take Louise with her and Louise learned on those occasions that she was a second class citizen through the prejudice of the children who lived in those houses. She was dark. The bosses' children were "light."

Eventually, a stepfather, whom Louise hated, came into their lives. Being a merchant marine, he was in and out of the house—a one-room apartment with kitchenette, that is. He provided food but no emotional support for the little girl whom he saw as an unwanted burden he had to tolerate in order to have Louise's mother. By the time Louise was twelve, he was gone, leaving the little girl with a ghastly view of relations both sexual and emotional between men and women. Louise's mother had to go on welfare because the jobs she could get did not pay for a subsistence-level existence.

Soon, Louise was a rebellious teenager. There were no supports for Louise's mother to help her deal with her. In Puerto Rico, her mother and Louise had had the values and support of a large community and family and the help given by their religion. In New York they had next to nothing. Hardly able to speak English, in an alien culture, Louise's mother was at a total loss. Louise was unmanageable. She had contempt for her mother and for most of the values any society considers good. By the time she was fifteen, she was a full-fledged drug addict with a baby.

For the most part, the father's family raised Louise's daughter, Colette. On a trip to Puerto Rico, she had a second child. Relatives of that baby's father took that child. Louise never saw her again. When she came back to New York, she continued to drink, drug, and deal and to prostitute herself. In the midst of it all, she had Juan who was "not quite right." Louise left the baby Juan with her mother for long periods while she pursued drugs, dealing, and prostitution. Occasionally, she had him with her, and when she did, she would often beat him and abuse him. He remembers being terribly embarrassed by his mother's drunken behavior, hating her, and running to his grandmother for solace. Grandmother tried her best with Juan. All she could do was to tell Louise she would kill her if she raised a hand to Juan again.

Could we even imagine anything good coming out of this mess?

After nineteen years of active addiction, which included a few stints in jail, Louise went into recovery. By this time, her two children, Colette and Juan, were nineteen and fifteen years old. Colette had come to live at different times with her grandmother and mother. Colette was well on the road to addiction and having children. In the next few years, two of Colette's children were taken away from her by the state and two died stillborn. Like her mother, Colette was a drug addict who dealt drugs and prostituted herself to support her habit. Meanwhile, Juan was still living with his grandmother and, as soon as he was able, was drinking uncontrollably.

Louise was in no position to do anything about them. All she could do was get clean and sober herself. The odyssey to recovery took thirteen years, even though she achieved her initial sobriety quickly. Through a 12-Step Program, Narcotics Anonymous, Louise became not only recovered but a powerful spokesperson and healer of other addicts in her own right. She was still only thirty- seven-years-old. She got a job eventually as a case manager for AIDS patients. She got an apartment. She spoke in prisons. She became a moral, self-actualizing dynamo. She was going back to school. She was going to get her GED, and, why not? her B.A., too. There was no telling how far Louise could go on the road to success. She was bright, beautiful, still young, and best of all, healthy.

Then tragedy struck. Louise was diagnosed with AIDS herself. This forced her to go on Social Security disability. The years she had invested in recovery now seemed futile. She had become a self-supporting, independent woman, and for what? Now she was sick and consequently dependent. Louise, nevertheless was one tough lady. She went after optimal health despite AIDS with the same guts and fervor with which she had pursued recovery. As she had for addicts, she became a spokesperson for AIDS causes. She appeared on television. She spoke to PWAs (Persons with AIDS) in prison. She still worked continuously on her recovery from addiction. Even as her strength and health began to fail, Louise fought on.

Sasha first met her when she became a client at an AIDS treatment center. At first, Louise hated the place because she had been a case manager for AIDS patients herself and a Lady Bountiful volunteering two afternoons a week for day treatment. Louise believed in the value of service to others. Now, she was reduced to the status of client and receiver of services rather than giver of them. This was a bitter pill indeed for this woman who had made so much of herself, who was so justifiably proud of rising out of poverty and addiction. It was hard indeed for her now to have to learn as much about accepting as she had learned about giving. And now, she had the added burden of dealing with the issues of her relationship to her mother and her children.

At this point, Louise's mother, at age ninety-two, began to fail. Louise took her to live with her in New York until she could find a senior-citizen home that was right for her. While they were together in Louise's little apartment, the two women made up their life-long quarrels. Louise enjoyed doing things for her mother. The mother was thrilled to be close again to Louise after so many years. When the mother moved to a senior home, Louise continued to visit and care for her. By the time the mother died, Louise and her mother had indeed cleaned up the debris of their past, and Louise was able to grieve without guilt.

As for the amends Louise needed to make to her children, Colette was still caught up in a life of drinking, drugging, and prostitution. Juan's situation was not so different; he was still suffering from not only organic deficits and the failures of nurture in his childhood but from active addiction as well.

This is what Louise taught us — how over the period of years before her mother became ill, she dealt with the problems of her kids.

First of all, she said, that because of the tragic childhoods she had given her children, she herself was their problem. Therefore, she couldn't be their solution. All she could do was be an example and set limits. The more they drank and drugged, the more she worked on her own recovery and health. She did not lecture or advise them. She just set the same limits she required for her own well-being for them. She did not let them live with her while they were actively using. When they begged for financial help, she gave them a sandwich and 12-Step meeting lists instead. All she ever said to them was that although she loved them, she could do nothing for them until they found sobriety. She refused to meet with them except in public places because being around active addiction threatened her own sobriety. Only by example did she teach them that sobriety was something to strive for, to value.

Colette came around first. Being a strong chip off the old block, she emulated her mother. Soon, she was on the path to recovery and a fulfilling life despite the fact that she had lost her two children. Out of that debris, the only satisfaction she and Louise had was that her children had been adopted together by good people. She also lost her husband to AIDS. By that time, she was recovered enough to see him through to the end. After so much loss, her mother was all she had and she feared deeply for her mother's health.

But at this point, Colette was sober, and Louise knew that now at last she could do something for her. After Louise's mother was comfortably ensconced in a nearby senior home, Louise had Colette come and stay with her. Mother and daughter lived together for several months just as Louise had lived with her mother. They got close. They went through the all the horror of the past, and as best they could, laid it to rest. It was a wonderful time for both. Colette and Louise together visited Colette's mother. Now, the three generations of women had a new relationship that was fulfilling to all.

Then, much to Louise's chagrin, Colette reported with excitement that she was pregnant, saying that she wanted to have one child in her life. Louise was appalled. The pregnancy seemed to Louise demeaning. A baby! No job! Welfare again! But now being a mature person, Louise managed to keep her reservations to herself—even if she was unable to meet the news with enthusiasm. For her part, Colette needed to have the child partly to make up for the children she had lost and partly as a diversion from her mother's deteriorating health. It was as if, with a new life, she was staving off her mother's upcoming death.

Colette was making plans for herself and her child. Although she was going to have to take welfare for a short period of time, she had herself enrolled in a GED program for after the baby was born. She had arranged for a babysitter as soon as she could get a job. Her mother's daughter, she said, "I'm smart and I can learn, and my little girl and me are going to have a good life—and I'm having my tubes tied right after the baby is born."

By now, Louise was beginning to suffer from the liver disease and other opportunistic infections that augur the end stage of AIDS. Although not happy about Colette's choice, she did not let it interfere with their loving relationship that was now that of two equal women not just mother and daughter. As Colette's pregnancy got more obvious, Louise began to fail more and more. She still had her relationship with her son to contend with. Her mother's death had brought that to a head.

Juan was so shocked by his grandmother's death that he went on a bender that ended with his being admitted to a psychiatric ward. For some reason, this was the crisis that made him at last embrace sobriety. Now that he was sober, Louise could come to terms with him. This was very difficult because mother and son really did not like one another. Louise had always been guilty and sad over his mental status. Juan had hated her for her abuse. To help Louise be able to treat her son lovingly, we helped her to write down all the things she hated about him and all the things she liked about him. In many cathartic sessions, she dealt with her ambivalent feelings. When she was able to meet with him without her negative feelings getting in the way, she told him how sorry she was for all the harm she had done him. He told her of all his resentments toward her. They both agreed that when she, Louise, died, Colette would manage the daily living problems that he had trouble with because of his mental status. Colette was very happy to do this for her brother since he would be her only family besides her child. By the time of the grandmother's death, Louise and her two children were able to grieve together in my office as a family, each giving support to the others. It was quite something to see them standing together, crying in a three-way embrace. In the next few months, Louise and her children negotiated the process of bereavement well.

There were still two more family issues Louise had to resolve before she could leave this life with a sense of peace and closure. We haven't mentioned her lover, Papo. She had had a volatile but very deep relationship with him for many years. Louise was unable, however, to have many loved ones in her life at the same time. It was as if she were only allowed so much love. If her children and mother were estranged, she could have her lover. If she was tight with Papo, she had to get rid of her children and her mother. Now, if she wanted a life that included her children, she had to get rid of Papo.

Finally, she announced she was breaking up with Papo, and they gave each other back their keys. Then the end came. Louise began having terrible nosebleeds and other symptoms that indicate liver failure. Hemorrhaging, she was admitted to the hospital where she soon went into a coma. In her careful way, she had left me a list of people to call. Papo's name was at the top of the list. I called him. He went straight to the hospital and, I swear, willed her to get out of that coma. We all thought Louise would not make it. After three days of Papo sitting by her bed with grim determination, she woke up. Even the nurses said it was a miracle.

Although she and Papo totally disagreed about her medical choices, they became close again. This pair—now in their late forties—emanated pure devotion. At this point, Louise was reconciled with her son, with her daughter, and with her lover. She was going home from the hospital. There was only one more person in her life she had an issue with.

Her granddaughter had been born five days before she was hospitalized. Everybody had been congratulating Louise on being a grandmother. Furiously she said to me, "I'm so sick of this grandmother @#@. I couldn't give a flying @#%@ about my granddaughter when my liver is failing, there's something bad in my lungs, and they're going to test me for stomach cancer." I said that, of course, she couldn't exactly welcome new life when her own was ebbing. We both cried and cried. She managed to go home only to be readmitted that night because of more hemorrhaging. The next morning, Colette brought the baby to the hospital. Louise was able to go down to the cafeteria to see her. Colette told her the baby was named Louise. People who saw them together told me that grandmother Louise looked like a little girl who had gotten more than she dreamed of on a Christmas morning. That afternoon when I came in, still like a little girl on Christmas morning, she said to me, "The baby, my granddaughter, she's perfect. She is really beautiful. And Colette really will take care of her."

Louise went into another coma and died a few days later with Papo sitting by her side. While he was out to lunch on the day before the end, I asked a priest to give Louise the last rites. I figured she was born a Catholic and might like to die one. When the priest came in, he said, "Oh, I gave her the rites last week. But I'll do it again if it'll make you feel better." Without ado he did so. I should have known Louise would have taken care of everything, including her relationship to her God.

Juan and Colette—well, Colette with Juan in tow—and Papo managed everything just as Louise's will directed. It is the only will I ever saw whose opening line said, "To my daughter Colette I give half of my teddy bears and all of my jewelry, (a few trinkets and one nice pair of earrings) to my son Juan I give the other half of my teddy bears and all of my furniture (a futon, a bed two chairs and a table with a TV), to Papo, my boy friend, I give all of my pictures of Puerto Rico, (framed magazine photographs.) I direct Colette to have my funeral in my apartment. I direct Papo to give my eulogy." Although materially, all Louise had to bequeath was teddy bears, her example of how to live, how to atone, how to die was of a value beyond price.

Not only to her children but to countless others.

The people coming to Louise's funeral filled her apartment and all the halls of her building. Many stood on the sidewalk outside. Her children, her lover, and her granddaughter in a stroller received all with grace and equanimity.

Juan and Colette found among Louise's papers a page from a coloring book, which depicted three children. She had colored them and put the names of Colette, Juan, and Rita. Colette told me that someday, when they had money, she and Juan would go to Puerto Rico to find her third child, Rita, and tell her that her mother was a good woman after all.

At least, when all is said and done, Colette, Colette's baby, and even Juan, have a chance of living fulfilling lives.

If Louise hadn't accomplished her recovery, it is doubtful they would have ever managed theirs.

Update: Juan is once again lost to addiction. Colette and her child are thriving. Colette told me, "I won't see Juan until he's clean." Who knows if Juan will ever recover? Perhaps with his mother's and sisters' example, he might.

Sometimes a child is lost—in part due to us—but there comes a time when there is nothing we can do about it. So be it, if we have at least done our best to rectify our mistakes. So be it.

Epilogue:
By the Skin of Our Teeth

Ever since World War II brought us the Holocaust, which taught us we could destroy 55 million people in twelve years, and the atom bomb, which taught us that we could destroy our planet with everybody on it in three or four hours, we've been nervous. To address this angst, Thornton Wilder wrote a wonderful play entitled *By the Skin of Our Teeth*, in which we see how we poor mortals have somehow survived calamity and total destruction from the Ice Age up to our own perilous times.

By the skin of our teeth we've managed, through the ages, to keep on having babies and raising families—despite famine, war, and weather. Bolstered by belief systems that were checklists for how to think and live, we knew that we were the elites of living creatures and that all we had to do to avoid hell and gain heaven was choose to be good rather than bad. With a little exemplary behavior and adoration, we could count on an all-good, all-powerful God who had made us just like Him to assure us eternal paradise, if not now, if not later, at least eventually.

Alas, starting in the sixteenth century, our feeling of existential safety was shattered by a number or narcissistic blows. Copernicus taught us that our planet was not the center of the universe, Darwin shocked us with unpleasant information about our ancestors, and Freud more recently showed us that we are not rational beings governed by values and choice but irrational beings subject to the inchoate drives of our unconscious.

Oh, to live back in the Middle Ages when even the poorest serf was sure that heaven was in the sky above him, our priests and our kings knew everything, and as long as we did what we were told and obeyed our betters, all would be well. We would go to paradise despite any misfortunes in our time on earth! For two thousand years or so, through the Judeo-Christian tradition, our Western world had found some comforting ways to run our lives. As long as we believed and stayed within our communities, our religions, our families, we had a blueprint for living. We knew what we were supposed to do according to our class, our race, our faith.

Then, in addition to Copernicus and Freud, we had to deal with the Renaissance, the Reformation, the Enlightenment, the industrial revolution, the American and French Revolutions, World War I, the Marxist revolution, World War II, the collapse of the Marxist revolution, and now the computer revolution—all laced with little to medium wars and no end of economic depressions. Through it all, by the skin of our teeth, we struggled to hold on to our faiths, our communities, and our cultures, But sometimes we get confused. Things seem muddled. Belief in anything is no longer simple. Like the serfs in the Middle Ages, some of us—even in our generation—lived with certain sureties. We grew up in communities where everybody was the same. Everybody knew what to do, whether they were Brahmins in Boston, store clerks in small towns, mommies in suburbs, or immigrant enclaves in cities. Raising children was not left up to the parents alone. Schools, churches, kin and clan all helped, custom and values all helped.

Our children and their children can never know the comfort and surety such an upbringing can give. Today, it seems every family has different rules. No church, synagogue, or ethnic group has all the answers any longer for their laities and landsmen. People intermarry. People belief-shop. Some run to fundamentalist religions and hold on to a narrow, deep, and sometimes cruel way of life to avoid emotional and mental chaos. Other people surf New-Age strategies, trying to become one with a benign universe. Some cling to science and what they can see and touch with implacable trust. Alas, while trying to make sense of the big questions and right and wrong, all anyone can count on is change.

The only place we're sure to see people coming together all across the country is shopping malls. There we parallel play at hunting and gathering objects for our homes, i.e., caves. The addiction rate in our country soars as we try to get rid of our anxieties. The voice of the community is the TV with its concomitant pap and violence and kindergarten newsbites.

All of this is a peculiar kind of tragedy. The tragedy of loss of custom and a sense of the rightness of the world. When people find their faiths diluted, their information sources reduced to first-grade readers, their ethics without muscle, they have to constantly question the way they manage their lives and families. They have to make up in one generation codes of behavior their ancestors took centuries to develop.

Now this is not all bad. Just as it is wonderful for a child who would be an orphan on the streets of Saigon to get adopted by a loving family and raised to have the best a child can have, it is wonderful for us to carve out new ways of living and arranging our families and our lives. Still, for adoption and forming new living systems to succeed, we have to recognize the loss of what once was. To overcome the tragedy of that loss we have to recognize there has been a tragedy in the first place. The adopted child, his birth parents, and his adoptive parents have to work through and understand the losses that initially brought them together. Two parents had to give up their biological child. That child will always have the wound of having been abandoned at birth. The adoptive parents will have to complete mourning for fact that they could not have their own babies. Once these losses are recognized, the joy and success of the adoption can be fully owned. If the shadow of the loss is worked through, there will be no dark corners in any of the participants' psyches.

So we parents and our children have to work through the knowledge that God may not be in His heaven, or even if He is, surely we know from our experience that not all is right with the world.

All this highfalutin thinking of the tragedy of not being sure, of not being able to count on even what we do know, and what it does to families, is a little beyond the ken of the authors of this book. Nonetheless, we believe with every fiber of our being, one thing: If everyone in the world would be nice to babies, that is, love them and give their parents the wherewithal to raise them, our world would become one without wars, without nine-tenths of its pain. If it became the worldwide custom not to let any baby suffer from emotional, physical, or mental deprivation, a population of intellectual, physical, and emotional giants would come into being. If babies are neglected or abused, they grow up to be angry adults and angry adults cause most of our evils—from crime to world wars. In some societies, the abuse of babies is a social norm. And those are very angry and warlike societies.

In this book we have tried to help parents like ourselves lose the silly wars with their adult children and thereby win their children's love, loyalty, and well-being. That way, the adult children can bring up their children in the best of all possible nurturing environment. And the more babies that grow up confident, loving, and capable, the better they will be able to cope with ice ages, warming climates, nuclear threat, and all the other ills our present day is heir to.

As we said before, loving parents make loving babies. Loving babies become loving adults. Loving adults create a loving society.

They are better at solving problems and surviving than are those crippled by emotional and physical deprivation in childhood.

It's all very simple really. If—by the skin of our teeth—we humans can be nice to our babies, our babies will grow up to be nice to us.

If we can be nice to our adult children, they will be nice to their babies.

And our DNA will have the best possible chance of survival.

And isn't that what all this is about?

Bibliography

Spotnitz, Hyman. *Modern Psychoanalysis and the Schizophrenic Patient*

Spotnitz, Hyman. *The Couch and the Circle*

Spotnitz, Hyman, and Phyllis Meadow. *Treatment of the Narcissistic Neuroses*

Spotnitz, Hyman. *Psychotherapy of Preoedipal Conditions*

Martelli, L. J., F. D. Peltz, W. Messina, and S. Petrow. *When Someone You Know Has AIDS*

Walker, Gillian. *In the Midst of Winter*

Kirman, William. *Modern Psychoanalysis in the Schools*

About the Authors

PAUL AVILA MAYER (CSW, PsyA) is a product of Hollywood and New York. He worked for many years as a free-lance writer for television and films and was co-creator, executive producer, and head writer of *Ryan's Hope*. He is now in his twelfth year in private practice as a psychoanalyst. He teaches at The New School for Social Research in New York City. He is devoted and profoundly grateful to his wife, Sasha von Scherler, and to his children and grandchildren. He was educated at Harvard (BA), NYU (MSW), and the Mid-Manhattan Institute of Psychoanalysis and Group Therapy (PsyA).

SASHA von SCHERLER (CSW) is a Renaissance woman. She works as a social worker, psychotherapist, actress, and writer. She was born in New York City and after a childhood of much travel has lived there all her life. She has been married to Paul Avila Mayer since 1958. They have three wonderful daughters, two great sons-in-law, and three enchanting grandchildren. Her education includes Vassar (two years), Yale Drama School (not invited back after her first year, a form of graduation reserved for the more original of the student body), CUNY (BA), and Hunter School of Social Work (MSW). She has studied at the Mid-Manhattan Institute of Psychoanalysis and Group Therapy, and the Center for Modern Psychoanalytic Studies.